About the author

I would consider myself to be 'ordinary' until I found I was the carrier of Partial Trisomy 9p, an extremely rare chromosome abnormality. My son, Charlie, had died as a result of the condition but, when Shelbie was born, I recognised that although Shelbie had the same condition, she appeared to be stronger than her brother. Although I had no formal medical training, I learned to undertake numerous complicated procedures to keep Shelbie at home. Despite the fact that Shelbie's life was expected to be numbered in months, I spent the next nineteen years fighting for my daughter's right to have a normal childhood, with the help of some family, a handful of key allies, and my deep faith. *Shelbie — Heaven's Borrowed Child* is my first book. I live in South Wales with my husband, Nick, six remaining children and three grandchildren.

This is a work of creative nonfiction. The events are portrayed to the best of the author's memory. While all the stories in this book are true, some names and identifying details have been changed to protect the privacy of the people involved.

SHELBIE
HEAVEN'S BORROWED CHILD

VICKI WILLIAMS
WITH JOHN TUCKER

SHELBIE
HEAVEN'S BORROWED CHILD

Vanguard Press

VANGUARD PAPERBACK

© Copyright 2023
Vicki Williams with John Tucker

A CIP catalogue record for this title is
available from the British Library.

ISBN 978 1 80016 947 0

*Vanguard Press is an imprint of
Pegasus Elliot MacKenzie Publishers Ltd.*
www.pegasuspublishers.com

First Published in 2022
Second Impression 2023

**Vanguard Press
Sheraton House Castle Park
Cambridge England**

Printed & Bound in Great Britain

Dedication

This book is dedicated to all of my beautiful children. Six of you had to grow up with a very different lifestyle to your peers. Without your often selflessness and patience some days just wouldn't have been possible. Charlie, I dedicate this to you also, because without your short presence I could never have been prepared for the journey that was coming our way. Of course, above all I dedicate this book to you, Shelbie Eloise. Even though you're no longer here in person. You taught us love, patience, acceptance, hope, strength, perseverance and above all how to live, truly live, to the max, regardless of obstacles and how to do that without words and mobility. This book could never have been possible if you hadn't opened up so many chapters and sent us on such an amazing journey.

Love always to all eight of you,
Mum.

Acknowledgements

My thanks to Amanda, Heather, Michelle and my family for the first days, months, years of Shelbie's start to life — without getting through that initial time, I wouldn't even have a story to tell. Mike 'T' and your family, Margarita and Jane, Gareth and Zoë, Gareth and Ellie. After Shelbs' 'promotion' I couldn't have even stood up, let alone written a book if you guys hadn't carried us in the dark hours leading up to Shelbs' 'promotion' and tirelessly after. Especially Gareth and Zoë, who didn't have a spare second in their day, yet made all the time in the world that we needed. Justin and Leah for helping us get out again and start living as Shelbs would have wanted. All the people we've met and come to love over the years from PICU and Little Bridge House and the nurses at home who all kept encouraging me to write about Shelbie's amazing life. Our *Born To Be Different* family, same to be said for you all, you never stopped believing in me portraying my precious child's life. Michelle and Linda from our old church, you believed I could do it and it inspired me with your enthusiasm. Of course, Nick, my teammate, you came into our lives and immediately you and Shelbs showed the definition of 'Daddy's girl' by her love for you and vice versa. You've pushed me and encouraged me all the way with this book and I thank you that we're still standing here together despite the odds. John Tucker, this book would never have been more than a very dusty journal left on a shelf if it hadn't been for you helping to write it. It didn't stop there, the advice and encouragement were above and beyond and I thank you wholeheartedly for that. I also thank your lovely wife, Lia, who gave me her husband's time for a while, but also stood me and Shelbs in good stead while she was Shelbie's social worker when she was a baby. And the last two, but most certainly not the least. God, our life and this book wouldn't have been what it is without your grace. Shelbie Eloise, this story most definitely wouldn't have been told without your lessons. You showed me that you don't need speech to speak a thousand words, illness doesn't need to define you and if you want something you keep pushing until you get there — even if no one else believes you can do it. You keep going until they're proved wrong. If a door's closed, you keep returning until it opens and if it doesn't you kick the life out of it until it falls down! Shelbs, your life was worth so much more than a few words and I pray that what people see when they read this is what we saw: pure strength, pure determination and pure love. To anyone not mentioned personally, it's not because you're not loved or thought of, the list is just too long and I need to stop somewhere, but thank you for believing I could do this, that I could somehow put into words the amazing life we were blessed to have with Shelbs and for walking this journey with us and,

like us, seeing that life with a disabled child can be lived, enjoyed, embraced, inspiring and above all can make us better people.

Foreword: November 2019

Once again, we'd spent the weekend filming for the TV programme, *Born To Be Different*. This time around it was a lot harder though, because it was the last time we would be taking part with all the other families. It's another chapter that inevitably needed to come to a close, but it's another closure we didn't want to make. Like leaving Little Bridge House. When we came home before Shelbie's funeral, we knew we could never return in the same way as we had before. Leaving there was something we were always going to struggle with but, as long as Shelbie was with us, we would cope, but now we were leaving because we had no choice. It would be hard to move forwards without that in our regular routine. We are allowed to go back for one final visit at some stage, but we aren't ready for that yet.

Coming to the end of filming is another closure we were being forced to make, another reminder of us not having Shelbs with us any more. The more things we have to move away from, the more distant we feel from our life as it was before. It wasn't our life for just a few months, it was spread over nineteen years and I found myself wondering who I actually am. And at this point in time, I don't know how to start finding out. I have been Shelbie's mum, and carer, for nearly twenty years. I was only in my early twenties myself when I had her, young and not planning ahead but just enjoying being a mum. I guess most people, as their children got a bit older, would begin thinking about starting a career or something. But I have been doing the mum job for nearly twenty-six years now and, although I have thoroughly enjoyed it, about ten months ago I started thinking about what I would do once Sophia started school. So I started working at Shelbie's school knowing I could fit it around all the children. And it worked well. I'm not against going back to working in the school, but I just don't know at the moment in which direction I'm feeling pulled. While in one breath I think maybe I should just wait and see where life takes me and take it slowly, in another breath I believe that you should go out and look for opportunities. Believe me, I know better than anyone that you can't take life for granted and, besides, taking things easy is just not me. I've never had that kind of life — it's always been fast-paced and I've crammed as much as I can into each day. It's the only way I am used to, the only way I know.

The doctor diagnosed both Nick and I with depression today. He said it was hardly surprising with the year we'd had, so we will start counselling and see if that helps us work through where we're at. It's not a bad thing, it just goes to show we are human, and we all have limits to what we can cope with in life. It's not a failure, it's not something to be ashamed of. It will shape us and maybe one day might even benefit someone else if at some point we can support others because of what we have experienced, what we have already lived though.

The filming actually went better than I could have hoped for, and we managed to enjoy it despite Shelbie not being with us. It taught me something, too. I had thought it would be inevitable that at some point Shelbie would be forgotten, or thought about less, but knowing what she means to other people has made me understand that she can never be forgotten. She was far too special and loved for that. I always said that once you met her you would never forget her, and now I truly understand it. She made such a huge impact that her memory will most definitely live on, maybe even after we — her parents — have gone, because her lessons are things people will still want to learn. Maybe that's where I need to be looking, finding a way of not only keeping her memory alive, but also her lessons. I was her voice for so long, and I'm still here, so there's no reason for me not to carry that message on for her. And she would have wanted that, I think. She knows she will never be forgotten or not talked about. We will keep her alive in a much more special way.

We went to a park and Ricochet, the company behind *Born To Be Different*, arranged for us to send off bubbles in Shelbie's memory. The funny thing is that we had visited that park years ago with some of the other children, Kalan, Mac and Cienna, and had said we would go back there one day with Shelbie, but we couldn't remember its name. So, of all the places we could end up, we found ourselves there, on this special day when we were remembering her and, while we were there, we came across a woman who is going to make a beautiful, personal and unique plaque for her memory bench. That can't have been a coincidence. Even though she is no longer with us in body, I believe Shelbie still had a say in what happened, and so she is still part of what goes on in our lives, day after day. In a very different way, maybe, but she's there, all the same. Always.

And this is her story.

Chapter One

In December 1993, Marc and I had a little boy — our first child — weighing in at eight pounds, four ounces, a nice healthy weight. We named him Rhys.

I'd been born in Grampian, Aberdeen, but we only lived in Scotland for about two years and were there because of Dad's work. We'd then returned to Little Stoke, a suburb of North Bristol (now in South Gloucestershire) which is where both of my parents had grown up. I was brought up in a Christian family, with my mum, Barb, my dad, Alan and my three brothers: Carl's the eldest of us, and then Matt and Paul followed me into the world.

I have so many happy memories of my childhood. My parents were definitely of the 'firm but fair' type, carrying threats through if necessary, and we had good rules and routine, but they were always willing to let us try things to learn whether they were good for us or not. I, of course, being a stubborn mare, felt everything that was bad for me was good for me, especially in my teenage years. I was an absolute madam, but they loved me regardless and I always felt that. I feel I had a fantastic childhood and a very loving family. I had both sets of grandparents living in the same area and we were all close, we saw all of our family regularly, and I think that's why my immediate family is so important to me now.

But I freely admit I was a trying teenager, and I left home at seventeen. I married Marc and moved to a place nearby called Stoke Gifford, which was about a twenty-minute walk from my parents' house. Unfortunately, they then moved to Coventry (again with Dad's work: he was employed by the Department of Transport) when I was about six months pregnant. It was hard not having them around, but they wrote and phoned regularly and we saw them most months. Matt and Paul went with them but Carl stayed in Little Stoke, so I saw a lot of him and kept a close bond. My grandparents have also always helped out, as did Aunty Sue. Aunty Sue wasn't a blood aunt at all, she was my mum's best friend and so was 'family' all the same, and I also had the support of Aunty Sue's five children, my 'cousins'. She had five children, of similar ages to us, and we all grew up together.

I had met Marc through friends. We all just hung out as a group and Marc and I got together from that. After going out together for six months we got married. I'd fallen pregnant with Rhys and, although my family never pushed me into anything, I guess I felt it was something I had to do. That's just how it was then, and we had the added expectation because of my Christian background. We bought a little two-bed flat and I thought we were doing OK for ourselves.

Just over a year later, in February 1995, I gave birth to another, very little, boy. Charlie weighed just three pounds, fourteen ounces. The midwife had said, while I was in labour, 'Oh, this is going to be a wee bunny,' but even she hadn't expected him to be quite so small. He wasn't breathing when he entered the world so had to be resuscitated. It felt as though I waited a lifetime for him to breathe — and even when he did, I don't remember hearing a cry.

The doctor came over and said, 'Your baby is very poorly, we need to get him to SCBU [the Special Care Baby Unit, as it was called then]; you can hold him briefly.' I did so for just a few precious seconds before he was whisked away. I was left in the delivery suite with many questions and no baby.

The doctor returned a while later and explained that she would be looking after Charlie as they were trying to work out why he was so small when he was full term. She questioned me about the pregnancy and my health through it. Had there been any problems? Was it a normal pregnancy? No, there hadn't been any problems and, yes, it had been a normal pregnancy. No one had picked up on him being small, so I presume I must have measured correctly during the months I was carrying him.

Charlie had various blood tests, as did Marc and I. When Charlie was three weeks old — and still in SCBU — blood results revealed he had Partial Trisomy 9p, an extremely rare condition of which only about one hundred cases had been reported worldwide at that time. It was so uncommon they knew very little about it, but we were told that it was a chromosome abnormality and that I was the carrier. We were given about two pages of information to read — which was all that was available — but I couldn't understand what any of it meant as it was written for specialists, not for parents. We were told Charlie could have learning difficulties and end up going to a special needs school. He was tube fed for the first few weeks, and then went on to a special premature formula via a bottle. It was painful feeding him. He was having only thirty millilitres every three hours, but it was taking over two hours to get that into him.

Charlie came home after a month in SCBU but didn't stay very long; he was constantly in and out of the children's ward with diarrhoea and vomiting. He wasn't discharged from the midwife until he was ten weeks old, and that was only because he had managed to hit the five-pound mark and the midwife had commented that if she didn't discharge him then she'd still be visiting on his first birthday.

At each admission to the hospital or visit to the GP I would point out a hernia he had above his navel. No one seemed overly concerned, but I kept mentioning it all the same because it didn't seem to be going, and it looked quite big. At just over eleven weeks, Charlie had another bout of diarrhoea and vomiting, but this time when he vomited it was coming out dark green. In fact, it looked like faeces. I took him to the GP who told me to starve him. He said it wasn't faeces; it was just bile or phlegm. As Charlie was no better the following day the GP told me to give half-strength feeds and see how things went over the weekend.

On the Sunday morning, Rhys managed to swallow a two-pence piece and, although he wasn't distressed, I thought I'd better get it checked out anyway. So, I took the boys off to the emergency department at Southmead Hospital with Marc and my cousin, Mike. Rhys was fine, but I asked the nurse if someone could also check Charlie over and she got him rushed through. I decided Rhys may be better off outside with his dad so I took him out to the car where Marc was waiting. By the time I got back to the cubicle Charlie was surrounded by doctors and nurses, inserting a cannula, taking bloods, and doing observations. They also put him straight on a drip. Once he was stable, they sent him over to his usual ward.

It was all so scary.

Once we were on the ward and I'd explained everything that was going on, the doctor told me they'd referred Charlie to a gastroenterologist because of his hernia. The gastroenterologist turned up from Bristol Children's Hospital within hours and explained that Charlie's hernia had dropped from his stomach down to his testicle and cut off his bowel: he was, in fact, 'pooing' out of his mouth. This is what I had tried to explain to the GP, and this was to be my first experience of a doctor not listening to me. Little did I know at this point that it would be the first of so very many.

Charlie was transferred from Southmead to Bristol Children's Hospital, and a few days later had an operation to correct the damage inflicted by the hernia. The results were amazing. A child who had hardly opened his eyes before, and who had just seemed to 'exist', was now looking around and gurgling. He was a different baby. My mum suggested that maybe this was the start of things to come, and I sat late that evening giving Charlie a bottle. The surgeon came in to see him and was happy with his progress.

Charlie and I were cuddling, watching *ER* on TV, when Charlie fell asleep. I put him down in his cot, told the nurse I was off to bed and, as I walked past his room, I glanced through the window. He had woken up. His little eyes were following me and it was lovely to see him so alert. I went to go back in, but the nurse told me she would give him some more water, so I carried on to bed, blissfully unaware that would be the last time I would see him awake.

I went to bed but just couldn't settle. I watched TV, I tried reading, I was tossing and turning. I didn't know why, but I felt very uneasy. Hours later I'd eventually dropped off through exhaustion, only to be woken by the nurse.

She said urgently, 'Come with me, Charlie's had problems breathing.'

What I didn't realise was that Charlie had actually stopped breathing. I sat in a room opposite, looking at my little boy through a window and watched the doctors resuscitating him, not actually realising that's what was happening, not really understanding what was going on. This was all so alien to me. Despite their efforts, Charlie died in the early hours of twenty-seventh of April 1995. He was just twelve weeks old when he was promoted to Heaven.

The night before his operation, I'd been in the shower, and from seeing him so ill pretty much daily I'd prayed, 'Lord, if Charlie is going to spend his whole life in pain, then you need to take him.' And so He did. It's the hardest thing to swallow, but it was the right thing for God to have done: to spare him this endless pain.

I was just nineteen. I'll always regret to an extent not being by his side when he died. If I'd understood what was happening, I could have gone in with the doctors so that he didn't die without me, but I was just a scared nineteen-year-old who knew nothing at that point. I can't change how it happened, I can only be grateful that I was blessed for three months. Some parents don't even get that. I wondered if, perhaps, he was paving the way for Shelbie, making me fight much harder to keep her, having already known the pain of losing a child. Maybe he did that for his yet-to-be-born sister.

My greatest regret though is that I have almost no recollection whatsoever of Charlie's funeral. I remember being there, but only just. I remember the date — third of May 1995 — but that's about all. I know I had the music played on panpipes ('Nothing Compares To U') to walk him in but that is my only memory of the day. It was too painful, I suppose, but there are so many times when I've wished I remember it. It was his only special day, the last day we would be with him, and I can't remember it.

But I do have memories of the precious few times we had him well at home, and memories of what Rhys was like with him. He was amazingly gentle, apart from when he used to bounce the baby bouncer until I thought the baby would take off. And I remember how he used to call him 'Choggy', as he thought that's what we called him. There are a few memories of taking the boys for little walks and a picnic. There are only a handful of photos of him, but there are photos all the same, and they are precious.

I began to write poetry to express my feelings, and this is something I wrote for him. I called it *A New Journey (A Poem for Charlie)*.

A New Journey (A Poem for Charlie)

My life was only short here,
But worth every minute.
I couldn't have been more loved,
More thought of, more cared for.

I thank you all for making my days
As happy as could be.
For teaching me what life was really about,
What unconditional love really meant.

I see your tears — I have them too.
I feel your pain — it hurts me also.
But please know that just because our journey together had to end —
It doesn't mean that there's no journey to continue.

I'm on a journey a different way and I'll always be able to see you.
You go down your new road now with pride —
We can always meet at the end.

I'll watch over you, you go now and set yourself free.
Feel no guilt — just keep loving the way you loved me.
I must say you make me proud,
I'm just glad I was able to know you.

Search deep within your heart and know in there I'm alive,
I'll always be smiling, I'll always be there.
We're closer than you may believe —
Our journeys not much different.

Only a few pages have covered the beginning and end of Charlie's short life, but that's just it: his life was so short, but so, so precious.

Thank you for spending time with me and letting me be your mum, Charlie, if only for such a short while. I love you.

Chapter Two

A twenty-week scan in pregnancy: so exciting for any parent.

After Charlie I'd had two more children, both of whom were healthy. Connor was born in April 1996, just a year after his brother had been promoted, and Courtney in July the following year. Both clocked in at over six pounds — nice, healthy weights.

After the midwife had carried out some checks she said, 'I'm just going to ask the consultant to come in. It's nothing to worry about.' Despite this being my fifth child, her words weren't very reassuring. The consultant had a look at the image and asked if we could go into another room for a chat. The baby was alive and was a girl, but that's all we knew at this point. He said there was some fluid on the baby's head and, that as her head was an unusual shape, he wanted to do further tests. I declined, arguing that whatever was going on with my baby would be dealt with when she was born.

He advised a termination.

I refused, and he became a little agitated and abrupt. 'So you'd rather bring a child into the world with brain damage?' he said, brusquely. 'She might not even survive the birth.'

My response was simple. 'God will be the judge of that.'

He just kept going on about a termination, stating my child might not have any quality of life but, as I wasn't going to back down, we were going around in circles. Eventually the midwife put my point across and it seemed to be accepted. Discussion over. I went back for a scan a week later. The fluid seemed to have gone and the pregnancy continued as normal — well, as normal as anything could be with Shelbie involved. She managed to loop a foot in my rib, causing bruising and a lot of pain!

I went into labour full term, and had a normal delivery. As soon as she was born, though, I looked at my new baby and knew something wasn't right. Although she weighed more than Charlie, she was still only five pounds. I asked the midwife to get a paediatrician. He came in and said nothing was wrong, and then asked why I thought there might be. I explained that she looked like Charlie, there were a lot of similarities, but more than anything I just felt it. He still insisted there was nothing wrong, so I just shut up, too tired to argue.

Our baby girl was born on twenty-ninth November 1999, and we named her Shelbie Eloise. At that time, we didn't realise that the name would literally be music to my ears. I sing her name, I put her name into stories when I tell her them, and my heart flutters whenever I hear it. I am just so proud to be the mother of Shelbie Eloise.

After a while we were moved to the maternity ward and I was telling every midwife that went past that there was something wrong with my little girl, but no one seemed to listen or agree. So, I asked for Dr Peter Lunt, who had been Charlie's geneticist, to review Shelbie, and he agreed to come the following day. Meanwhile, the midwives were telling me there was nothing to worry about, which I feel prevented me from bonding with Shelbs. I was so confused. I felt like I was being told to love this particular child that I did not know.

The midwife I saw the following day was fantastic. She just listened. She didn't try convincing me either way and that was so much what I needed. I had hardly held Shelbie since she was born, and she had spent the night in the nursery because at this point, I didn't know who I was meant to be loving. Dr Lunt came in and asked what my initial instincts were. I told him I thought she had Partial Trisomy 9p, like her brother Charlie. He agreed that she had the same dysmorphic features and would confirm it with a blood test. He did say though that Shelbie appeared a lot tougher than Charlie; physically she was a lot stronger, and she seemed to just have a fight in her. If only he knew how right his words would prove to be!

As soon as I had been told what I already knew, that gush of love came and, my goodness, it came in floods. I think it was relief that I knew who she was now, and also a little guilt for pushing her away at the start. I kept kissing her, saying, 'I'm sorry I didn't love you yesterday.'

It was three weeks later when Dr Lunt rang to confirm what we already knew. This was the start of Shelbie's life with Partial Trisomy 9p.

In the meantime, Shelbs had been referred to a cardiologist to see if she had the same heart problems as Charlie, which is how it appeared to me. The night before the appointment, when Shelbs was just four days old, I'd noticed that she seemed to be holding her breath. She would go blue, and I'd have to flick her on her chest or her feet for her chest to noticeably move again. I mentioned this to the doctor and he said it was common for new-borns to do this when they have wind. I explained that it was more than blue lips from wind, as her entire face seemed to change colour. I'd had five children by this time and I knew a windy face when I saw it. He didn't really respond to that so I left it, wondering if perhaps I was overreacting because of Charlie.

He gave Shelbie an ECG and an echo scan which revealed a small atrial septal defect and a patent foramen ovale. She had a hole in the heart, and one of the vessels to the heart was narrow. I think that's what he said it meant. She was started on two diuretic drugs and was to be reviewed in six months, and at this we were sent on our way.

A week later Shelbs had diarrhoea and vomiting and was looking quite grey, and furthermore was still having these episodes of so-called "trapped wind". I took her to the GP who put her straight on oxygen and told the receptionist to call an ambulance. The receptionist returned, saying the ambulance would be about half an hour.

'This child won't be here in half an hour. I need a blue light call now.'

I realised this was serious, but again it was all so new to me. At this point I still believed that if a doctor says it's black, it's black. I wouldn't have questioned it.

Shelbs was rushed to hospital. I felt sick and numb at the same time. She was on monitors, one of which kept alarming, and the nurses looked worried; this much I could work out for myself. They kept flicking Shelbie's tummy and feet when the monitor went off, and the doctors and nurses were talking amongst themselves, but I understood nothing of what was being said or what was going on. I just knew it was serious. It's quite funny really because as the years went on and I'd started to learn more and more medical terminology, the doctors who'd stand in Shelbie's room discussing things, started stepping outside when they realised I'd come to learn their language. This always did make me chuckle. Back then though, all I knew was that this was serious, I just kept praying. 'Please God, don't let her die as well.'

A doctor introduced himself as Dr Stanley. He remembered me from Charlie. He even described what Charlie looked like. I was so touched, as it had been nearly five years since Charlie had been with us, and I also felt comforted that Shelbie's doctor was someone who had cared for her brother. He explained that Shelbie was having apnoeas — periods of not breathing — but they didn't know why. She had bloods taken, urine tested, etc., looking for an infection or some kind of answer. Shelbie was kept on oxygen and seemed to stabilise. They also discovered around this time that she had hypothyroidism so was started on thyroxine.

This was the start of many hospital visits with either diarrhoea and vomiting or chest infections. They didn't work out why she was having the apnoeas, but was referred to a Professor Fleming. At our appointment he showed me how to stimulate Shelbs when she had the episodes, and how to resuscitate if that failed. He also put her on an apnoea alarm so I would know when she wasn't breathing, which meant I could care for the other three children rather than be sat over Shelbie's pram or cot watching and waiting for every breath.

I thought the first three months would be the worst. If we just got past the age at which Charlie died, then I would relax. But that didn't happen, of course. I came to realise that life with Shelbie wasn't about relaxing. She always had various viruses and bacterial infections, and even when she didn't have bugs she always seemed to be vomiting. She was bottle fed but didn't find it easy, so the dietician at the hospital put her on a special Haberman bottle which controlled the flow and made it easier for her to suckle.

She was still vomiting though, and this would cause her to aspirate, meaning the vomit would go back into her lungs causing chest infections and increasing her apnoeas. We met her respiratory consultant, Huw Thomas, on that first admission and he would be her consultant all the way through.

A chest infection at four months had resulted in us not being able to get Shelbie off the oxygen so she came home on it. During this admission, though, the nurses helped me to start weaning her onto solid food. So natural for other children, but this was a big milestone for Shelbie.

To make things worse, around this time Marc left. It had all proved too much for him, and either the death of a child or having a sick child gives pretty poor statistics for marriages lasting. Put the two together and there's really not much chance at all. Once we'd had Charlie, Mum and Dad had moved back from Coventry to support us and that had been a great help. But when Charlie died, I think, maybe because of our age, neither of us knew really how to get past it as a couple and the cracks started to show. I took my vows very seriously though and I don't agree that it's "just a piece of paper" so I continued trying to work at our marriage. But after seven years of married life and three more children, for various reasons it all fell apart. When Shelbie came along that was the end of it, really. When she was just four months old Marc left us and for a while — before Nick came along — I pretty much did it alone. My family were of course very supportive at the time, and I'd moved back to Little Stoke a few years earlier, but with Marc gone it was me and my four beautiful children. So life carried on, although now it just the five of us: Rhys, Connor, Courtney, Shelbie and me.

Shelbie's vomiting continued and at about six months the doctors recommended tube feeding, which I refused. I was petrified, and also wrongly believed that she would have to stay in hospital for it as I hadn't realised she could be tube fed at home. That hadn't been an option for Charlie. But then again, I also hadn't realised you could have oxygen at home, yet here we were. I was told it was natural to feel anxious and that I would be just fine. Are you kidding me? I was still getting used to her being on oxygen!

Mum and Dad were amazing at helping with the children, as was my cousin, Mike — one of Aunty Sue's children — and his partner, Ruth. Mike's not a blood relative, as I've said, but it's not just about blood, is it? That's not what makes a family, as I have realised more and more over the years. Mike had spent a lot of time with Charlie so understood better than most how hard it was for me. In fact, he'd been looking after Rhys the night Charlie died.

My oldest friend, Michelle, spent a lot of time at the hospital with me in those early days. I also had the support of the Lifetime Service to whom Shelbs was referred by the midwife. They would do bloods at home and come to appointments with me, taking notes and ensuring I had understood what was going on. They had a psychologist too who offered support which proved very useful for Rhys who was, shall we say, a very "full on" child.

We also had Jessie May nurses who offered a few hours' respite each week which was much needed. At the beginning of Shelbie's life, we were allocated a social worker for support and I also had a fantastic health visitor. That social worker left and we had another one called Lia who would go on to be a huge support. I wouldn't have got through some of the tough times without her. Lia made a referral for us to a children's hospice, Little Bridge House, near Barnstaple. I was quite scared about this but Lia reassured me, convincing me to visit and just have a look around. It took a while to actually get to see the place because every time a date was set, Shelbs would go into hospital, and it was a two-hour drive to get there so it wasn't easy to arrange. But Lia did arrange it, and took Shelbie and myself there to meet everyone. Little Bridge House would go on to become an important part of our lives.

By around the age of six months, Shelbie was recognising certain people by touch. She couldn't see very well due to having ptosis — droopy eyelids — but she knew my dad by his beard, my mum by her glasses and me by my nose stud. She would feel your face to work out who you were and once she'd established this, she knew who was holding her. We also started encouraging sitting with the support and advice from the physio at the special needs tots' group, we attended. She eventually learned to sit up for about thirty seconds, which is quite a long time when you're counting, but would often lose this ability when she got ill and we would have to start at the beginning all over again.

This, special needs tots' group, was run at the hospital. They would show us ways to help with rolling, crawling and communicating by using Makaton sign language, and the support from the leaders and other parents was immense. One day at group, when Shelbs was about nine months old, the leader handed out some leaflets. A production company called Ricochet were looking for children who had additional needs for a programme they were planning to film. As a group we had a little discussion about it, and I put the leaflet in Shelbs' bag but thought nothing more of it at the time.

A few days later I was clearing Shelbie's baby bag out and came across the leaflet. I couldn't decide whether to call or not. I had wanted to hide when Charlie was diagnosed, not because I was ashamed of him but because I couldn't face people's opinions. I realised that unless these "opinions" were faced head on, and challenged, nothing would ever change. Until people like me, people who had a voice, stood up and argued back in the face of criticism no one would understand these kids' side of the story. And the long and short of their story is they just wanted to be accepted, to be happy and to enjoy life to the full as is their right, the same as anyone else. So I called the number to get some information. They explained they were doing a one-off documentary with several families to try to get the world to understand what life is like with a disability and to empathise with children and parents alike. I thought, 'Yeah, this is the loudest I can shout: through TV.' So began the start of what was to be a long journey filming for a programme called *Born To Be Different*. What started as a one-off became a long-running series which ran for many years, following the lives of a group of families as their children grew up.

Back at home, my older kids were spending a lot of time with my mum and dad and I could see a change in their behaviour. Courtney was nearly three, Connor four and Rhys six, and this was a lot for three so young to just accept as a part of everyday life. At the time I felt that, although Mum and Dad were fantastic with having the children and being sensitive to their needs, the best thing for my children was to be with me, wherever that was. I thought at first it was best that they be away from whatever was going on in the hospital and be cared for by close family, keeping their life and routine familiar. But the reality was that things weren't the same and that they would need to adjust to that too, but if they had Mummy by their side, they would know that, whatever was changing, I was still there with them. They had lost so much already. I went to check on them all one night before I went to bed and Courtney was nowhere to be seen. I eventually found her curled up in the foetal position under her bed, a place she felt safe, as my health visitor would later comment. That was when I realised that I'd got it wrong. They all needed to be with me and Shelbie, wherever we were.

So I started taking them to the hospital and, although it may not sound ideal, we were all together, which was important. Perhaps more importantly, they saw for themselves what was going on with their sister, rather than not really having a clue and imagining all sorts of things which were probably far worse than the truth of the matter. And I was right to do this. I noticed they all started settling down, and this new routine became their norm. I would drop the boys at school and Courtney to playgroup, and when playgroup wasn't on, she would come to the hospital with me. Weekends and school holidays were spent at the hospital. We were all together, and we could still play games wherever we were. My sister-in-law, Heather — who was married to Carl at the time (although they'd separated and she was staying with me) — and family friend, Amanda, would help out with sitting in the evenings so I could be with Shelbie. I'm not sure I could have done it without them.

Our new routine was much healthier than trying to maintain our old life. I suppose I never really appreciated how much all our lives would change. It's not just about the affected child. I also had Rhys who had been diagnosed with ADHD (and I believe has Asperger's although this has never been confirmed) and he struggled more than anyone with change. There were many people that helped my children feel some security and they were also the support that kept me going, but I still felt immense pressure and when all was quiet it was me who would sit and worry, me who had to make major decisions for all four of them. And that was hard sometimes, and lonely too. I don't think I did an awful job with the children, but I feel I could have done better at times. It was physically draining running around after four little ones, and emotionally draining too. Without my family and friends, I'm not sure where I would be right now. They listened, they laughed with me and they cried with me too. Amanda, Heather and Michelle were my rocks.

Just before Shelbie's first birthday she developed RSV — respiratory syncytial virus. This attacks the respiratory system and, as Shelbie already had breathing problems, she suffered really badly and ended up in PICU — the Paediatric Intensive Care Unit, then in the old building at Bristol Children's Hospital which was familiar to me because that was where Charlie was when he died (Shelbie's later visits to PICU were in the new building). She was in for a couple of weeks, making it back to her usual ward just days before her birthday.

This was my first experience of intensive care and ventilators and also of being told, 'She's critical, the next X number of hours/days are crucial,' as her left lung had collapsed and so was cause for concern. By this point, though, a lot of the monitors, alarms and tubing had become a lot more familiar to me as a lot of it we used at home or when she was on the general ward. Shelbie was put on CPAP — continuous positive airway pressure — and she pulled through. Whenever she was ill after that it was always the left lung that was a concern. But if her breathing was OK her diarrhoea and vomiting would be back. She rarely seemed to get a break in those first few years of her life.

After this visit to PICU Shelbie refused to take solids any more. We tried every which way to encourage it but speech and language therapists felt that the trauma of the ventilator tubing in PICU had caused psychological damage too. I felt gutted. Eating solids was something she could do and now it had gone, like the sitting up whenever she was ill. One thing she did still love though was her bottle and sucking her thumb, and her thumb sucking was something no one could take from her.

When Shelbie was nineteen months old, I had her dedicated. I wasn't saying she would grow up to be a Christian and love God because that's not my decision or something I could or would control as she got older. However, I feel a dedication is more thanking God for this precious life and stating she would grow up to be taught about God. She was in hospital when her special day — first July 2001 — arrived, but was stable enough for me to take her out for "day release". It was a lovely day, and extremely emotional when Dad read the poem I had written for Shelbs, he cried, which then made me cry. But what a special day it turned out to be. Wow, who would have thought Shelbie was already a year and a half old, and so clever and so strong!

This is the poem I wrote for the day. I called it simply *Shelbie's Prayer*.

Shelbie's Prayer

I pray that as this child grows
You will give her the strength to walk, talk, smile and have hope.
Even if this journey is a short one
I pray it's as happy and pain free as it can be.

And if she can't walk and talk
I pray that this will be accepted by all and
That the love she has to give will be returned without ignorance.

No matter what we want, our lives have been decided
And we have to accept what we've been given.
That doesn't mean we can't enjoy it.

If this child could talk, I'm sure she would tell you —

I won't suddenly get better.
I may do a bit better but I will always have my illness,
So please accept that and love me for who I am,
Not for what you may have wanted me to be.

I'm not less worthy than the next child,
Just a bit different maybe, but I'm happy
So please be happy with me and love me like I love you.

In the summer, and during bouts of vomiting and aspirating, the question of tube feeding was brought back up. Another mum on the ward started chatting to me. We got on so well, we became really good friends. Her son had the same problems with feeding and she'd gone through the same emotions, so with a lot of discussion and encouragement I finally agreed and trained to tube feed Shelbie. She started off with a nasogastric (NG) tube but she was still allowed her bottles so it was not all bad. We had the fun of passing new tubes through her nostril and into her stomach and if she pulled the present one out (or vomited it out) it wasn't pleasant to start with but eventually I made a game out of it and it was the first time

I remember hearing Shelbie laugh. I was blowing raspberries on her neck and singing silly nursery rhymes while trying to discreetly pass this tube without too much fuss and she started giggling at me. It had only been months previously that she had started smiling so these things were heart melting for me.

Shelbie was still aspirating though, despite the NG tube, so when she was about two years old, Dr Thomas felt it safer to stop the bottles completely. While I agreed with the decision, I felt cheated that she couldn't feed herself. Shelbie loved her bottles. Whenever she was ill the doctors would come in and, as they knew her well, they would evaluate how bad she was by whether she was still feeding or not. In fact, when she had that first visit to PICU I remember the doctor asking me how she was in herself, and then saying, 'And what about her bottle? Is she still taking that?' When I said she wasn't, he actually replied, 'Oh, she must be bad if she isn't even having her bottle.' Whatever else was happening with her, she would always have the comfort of the bottle.

The other kids loved it when Shelbs came home with her NG tube. They enjoyed helping to feed her, and I felt it was good for them to be involved as much as possible in a positive way. Being solely tube fed didn't work either, though, as she was still vomiting and aspirating. Dr Thomas decided the next step was a fundoplication (a procedure where the stomach is wrapped around the gullet, making it, in theory, impossible to vomit). While Shelbie was under general anaesthetic, they were also going to insert a PEG tube so that she could be fed directly into her stomach, and to have ptosis surgery for her droopy eyelids. Rather than risk several general anaesthetics it was felt better to have it all carried out under one, so we awaited a date. On top of that, the cardiologist also decided he wanted a cardiac catheter done, which is an exploratory procedure, so Dr Thomas also decided to do a bronchoscopy while she was unconscious. He didn't expect to find anything, but just took the opportunity as it arose. The doctors returned from theatre quite surprised, as they, in fact, had found something. Shelbie had trachea and bronchomalacia which meant her windpipe was floppy, which meant it sometimes closed over. This explained her failure to breathe, she was 'plugging' off. The outcome of this was Shelbie would always remain on oxygen and might need a tracheotomy and end up with a tracheostomy.

I was beginning to learn at this point never to take anything for granted, especially where Madam Shelbie was concerned. I thought, 'Well, we'll always have the O_2, but she's doing OK with it so we'll just carry on.'

After Shelbie came out of theatre she didn't seem quite right, but I had to leave her for a bit as, the week before, the little friend she had made in hospital had died and today was his funeral. This little friend was someone Shelbie had met a year before, and they had spent a lot of time together. If they were ill in hospital at the same time — which was often — the nurse would put them in adjoining rooms so that they could see each other through the glass. We went for walks together, to the park, out for lunch, little picnics. I became really good friends with his mum, whom I'll call Jane. We supported each other and made each other laugh. We stayed in hospital with the kids one night and sat in the parents' lounge with a few glasses of wine and had a girlie night, and the nurses said they would call if we were needed. I had to be there with her and her husband on this day; their baby was just two years old when he died. Straight after the funeral I headed back to the hospital and, as soon as I saw Shelbie, I knew something was wrong. I voiced my concerns, but no one seemed to share them with me; no one seemed to be listening. Then she went into respiratory distress, at which point everyone started listening! It was not the day I wanted it to be, seeing her like this, and I was angry that it wouldn't have got to that point had I been listened to.

A few months later Shelbie went in for her triple operation. The fundoplication was quite a big operation so I knew she would be going to intensive care afterwards to give her the best chance of a good recovery, but she did really well and was only in intensive care for a week. I will never forget Shelbie leaving PICU to go back to her usual hospital because it was the first time she had ever seen daylight properly. She was fascinated, looking around everywhere, but also looking a little confused at the same time. All I could look at, were her beautiful, sparkling blue eyes. It made me realise just how closed her eyes had been before the operation. They made her face light up. She was so pretty. And, of course, now she could see all the people she knew and loved for the first time — the people she had only known by touch and by sound before.

Those first two years of Shelbie's life were largely spent on Badger ward, part of the Woodlands Children's Unit at Southmead hospital, and the staff on the ward are the people who helped get us through. We built relationships with the cleaners, nurses, play workers, all the people who worked there. They shared laughter, heartache and tears with us. They used to wind me up all the time, getting students to style Shelbs' hair in a certain way I wouldn't like, or getting an outfit from the cupboard that I'd hate, knowing when I came in, I would go mad. But it gave us all some giggles and those poor students…

In a funny kind of way, these were probably the best of days because the staff knew Shelbie so well and knew how poorly she was so helped me manage to laugh as much as I could. I could phone anytime, day or night, and someone who knew her would be there to reassure me. If we had a new doctor, the nurses could help explain what did and didn't work for Shelbie. A parent's explanation often seemed to fall on deaf ears, so it was nice having professionals in your corner. It was a small unit with only two wards but it worked well for us and it was so comforting having that familiarity of place and staff.

When she was about two and a half years old Shelbie moved from the baby ward to the "big girls'" ward. This was probably more of a change for us than it was for Shelbs, but over time we grew to love the staff. Shelbie loved being part of the Woodlands Unit at that hospital, and it was like having a family of nurses who really loved her and her cheekiness. This "new" life we had wasn't all bad, and Shelbie's character and zest for life were already shining through.

Precious Child (A Poem for Shelbie, July 2001)

I woke up this morning not wanting to face yet another day.
Then I remembered—
I have my health,
I have the use of my legs,
I can express my emotions
And I can breathe with no pain.

These things you cannot do
Yet somehow you are stronger,
You still smile, you still try,
You keep going, just grateful to be alive.

Did I ever say I'm so proud of you?
Did I let you know you're so loved,
And these are the reasons you make it worthwhile,
The reasons I want to keep going?

You turn a frown into a smile,
A cloud into sunshine,
A doubt into hope,
Tiredness into strength
And heartache into a precious lesson—
That is why you're so special.

Chapter Three

Shelbie came home a short while after her "fundo" surgery. We were warned by her surgeon, Miss Cusick, that she could continue retching for up to six months after surgery, but she didn't — it stopped immediately. No more vomiting! Shelbie was like a different child and looked really well; she no longer sounded chesty all the time and her character really started to come out. She found things funny and was starting to come alive.

My friend, Jane, supported me unbelievably despite what she was going through and decided I needed a man in my life. She and her husband set me up on a blind date with someone they knew named Nick. She had told him all about the children and Shelbie's additional needs and he still wanted to meet up, so I guessed he must be a pretty decent bloke. We met and got on really well right from the start, and the first time he met the children he was very natural with Shelbie. He wasn't uncomfortable around her at all. Who knew then he would end up being her daddy, and the only daddy she would ever know? Marc saw the children infrequently (and I don't think he ever took his visits seriously) but he never had a connection with Shelbs so she never knew anyone as her daddy except for Nick.

Around the time of meeting Nick, Shelbie, after lots of encouragement and persuading, had started rolling completely on her own. Discovering that she could get to places quickly she then mastered the art of breaking whatever she could get her hands on.

Three months before her third birthday I was chatting to my brother, Paul, and his wife, Emma. Shelbie had been sat in her chair eating rainbow drops. Yes, actually eating! We'd also persevered with that and she ate when it suited her. She wouldn't tolerate a meal but loved strawberry sundaes and mainly sweet stuff which meant she could have treats with the other children. After she'd eaten her sweets I lay her on the floor for a roll around — where she loved being the most — when I noticed her leg twitching. I chuckled, thinking she had a trapped nerve, but as I picked her up, she continued to do it and I noticed her arm doing the same. I turned to Emma, who has epilepsy, and said, 'She's fitting, isn't she.' Emma agreed that's what it looked like, so I called for an ambulance.

At the hospital the doctors said they would allow for one seizure as it was a hot day and it could have been a febrile convulsion, but after more seizures and an EEG she was diagnosed with epilepsy. Dr Stanley monitored this and started her on anticonvulsants. Over the years Shelbie suffered five different types of seizures, obviously — one just wouldn't be enough! She had tonic clonic seizures where her body would jerk; paralysis fits, where she was awake and aware of her surroundings, but couldn't move (I struggled with these the most because her eyes would say, 'Help me'); gelastic fits which was uncontrollable laughter; atonic fits which are drop fits, so if she was sitting up she would just drop forwards uncontrollably with little response; and apnoeic seizures, where she stopped breathing until emergency meds would kick in and she would breathe again. These were similar to the breathing difficulties she had when she "plugged off". Shelbie had a floppy airway, so when it would temporarily close over, she wouldn't be able to breathe, and this is what is meant by plugging off as, like a plug, it would get in the way of her being able to breath. Also, when she was ill the mucus would act as a plug which would cause breathing difficulties, but this was more obvious to determine. When it was because of her floppy airway, it was sometimes hard to ascertain whether it was that or in fact the seizure. Most of the time these were controlled but everything was dependent on how her general health was.

Six months after Shelbie's operation she decided to prove everyone wrong and not only start retching again but go one better, vomiting as well. To this day no one knows how or why. Miss Cusick said sometimes the fundo can loosen over time, but she checked Shelbie years later and said it was as tight as the day she did it so it made no sense. Our response to Shelbie doing what she shouldn't do commonly became, 'Trust Shelbie…' She was defiant, and if you said she couldn't or shouldn't do something she most definitely would do it and doubly so. Actually, thinking about it, she sounds very much like me in that respect!

Shelbie celebrated her third birthday at home, the first time she was home for her big day, so we had a little family tea with my mum and dad. Nick had moved in around the time the vomiting started and we talked about buying a family home together. After looking at various areas we settled on South Wales, and a few weeks after our birthday celebration we had the keys to our new house. Mum and Dad had the children overnight and Nick and I stayed in the new house, ready to unload the van the following morning, with just a quilt, a TV, an Indian takeaway (but no cutlery) and our Staffie, Kira. The following day, with the help of both sets of parents, we moved in, and it felt like home immediately.

Just a month later, though, Mum rang me to tell me Dad had been admitted to hospital as he just hadn't been feeling right: he was having trouble moving one side of his body properly. We dropped the kids at Amanda's and rushed to Southmead Hospital. Dad was going for scans and was a bit tearful, and it was hard to see him crying. We stayed with him a while, then as it was getting late, we left to let him rest. On our way home my brother Matt rang, in tears. After various tests Dad had been told he had a brain tumour. We turned around and headed straight back to Mum's so we could all be together. After more tests we were told the tumour was malignant. We had about two years with him at most.

Dad knew everything. He was our family rock, and I couldn't believe he was going to be the vulnerable one now. I spent every day with him over the coming months. He had an operation to remove the tumour and they were happy that they'd got the best part of it. But just months later he had a seizure at home. He was rushed into hospital and not expected to survive. Thankfully, my eldest brother, Carl, was local, but Paul and Emma were on holiday and Matt was in London working. I had to call them to come home straight away. We all went to the hospital where they immediately let us in, despite it not being visiting hours. That, and the fact that the curtains were pulled around his bed, made me realise that things weren't good. Nurses do things subtly but over time, when you're living the hospital life, you tend to pick up on things others might not notice.

Dad did make it back home, but the tumour seemed to be back with a vengeance and he appeared a lot weaker. It was so hard to watch him deteriorate in front of our eyes, and he was so much more emotional after his operation and would cry about anything. Regardless of all this he never lost his sense of humour, we'd laughed and cried through so much as a family, but definitely managed a lot of laughter.

Once when Dad had been admitted to hospital — this time he was at Frenchay — we sprang a surprise family picnic. Mum told him she was taking him for a walk around the grounds and as they walked to the green, there we all were waiting for him and — surprise, surprise! — he cried, but he was so happy. You learn how to work around things when you spend so much time in hospital. There were countless occasions with Shelbie when I would take her for a walk to the green and let the children eat their lunch, so they had the treat of a little picnic. Or Nick and I would take Shelbie out on what we used to call "day release" if she was well in herself but was in hospital having IV antibiotics. We just had to ensure that we had her back for the next dose. There are ways to find some kind of normality if you know how to look for them and can plan that little bit better. It was a fantastic day with Dad and, while we were there, we told him that he was going to be a grampy again. He was over the moon. Nick and I had got engaged a few months before, and also Paul and Em were getting married, so there were a number of nice and positive things for him to focus on. After about five months following his diagnosis, though, he seemed to start to deteriorate quite quickly, and he had a few more seizures. Paul and Emma brought their wedding forward by a few weeks but he wasn't able to make it to the ceremony. He was too weak by then, but at least they managed to have some photos taken with him. At thirteen weeks, I'd lost the baby, just days before their wedding (in fact, Nick and I lost two babies quite close together). Dad died just two days after the wedding, with us all there around him. We had him only for six months after he first became ill in July 2003.

In the weeks before he was promoted to Heaven I realised, as I was sitting with him one day, that I hardly ever told him I loved him. I sat cwtching — cuddling — into him and told him how much I loved him. I knew then that there would never be another moment like this and that such opportunities were limited. Their wedding anniversary was just days before he died, but with my help he managed to sign a card for Mum.

It was so sad for us but fantastic for him. In all the time he was ill I never remember him once asking, 'Why me?' He just trusted that God would heal him, whether that be in Heaven or here on earth. He totally gave himself to God and kept his faith strong, as he had done our whole lives, whatever the situation. He was such a testament to what it is to be a Christian. I mentioned before that we grew up in a Christian family, and when I was about twelve, I became a Christian myself at a Billy Graham meeting. I was baptised at fourteen by our pastor and my dad, and I really wanted to follow my parents' example but I just let life be taken over with temptations. I strayed from the "church life" and when God took Dad, I'll admit that I was very angry. I know that every second of every day He knows best, but I'd completely lost sight of that back then. I guess I'd drifted after my ex-husband left, and felt that actually I was just fine on my own and didn't need to answer to anyone, not even God.

The night Dad died, Shelbie had to try and upstage him with a big fit which required a blue light, something she always seemed to enjoy very much. Unless the ambulance's lights and sirens were flashing and wailing it didn't seem worth her while so she'd do something to ensure she got her wish which usually revolved around a lack of breathing. It was on this admission that we realised that Shelbie made no effort to breathe if she received too much oxygen, so we had to ensure her sats were always below 100% as she had a hypoxic respiratory drive, which apparently is common with chronic obstructive pulmonary disease (although COPD is one of the few things she didn't actually have). Once we had Madam stable, we went back to the house to say goodbye to Dad before he was taken away. It was a crazy night, but so typically Shelbie.

Dad's funeral was amazing. The church was packed out and everyone who spoke about him mentioned his infectious smile. The same is always said about Shelbie, maybe that's where she gets it from.

A few months before we'd moved to our new house, Shelbie had started part-time at a special needs school, something she really seemed to love. She had started getting into the crawling position when she was about four and even made attempts to move forwards — Dad would have loved to have seen all this as he was so proud of all his grandchildren. Shelbs could also do a few steps backwards but, like everything else, as soon as she had learned it, she became ill and had to start from scratch. This happened a few times, after which she lost interest in trying. So, every now and again she would get into the crawling position although this only happened a handful of times over the years. She was still a top-notch roller though, and thankfully that's something that she never seemed to lose permanently. We knew how frustrated she would have been if she hadn't been able to get where she wanted when she wanted.

With the exception of short stays in hospital, Shelbie was spending a lot more time at home and life was "normal" now, although our normal was very different from everyone else's and largely decided by Shelbie. Six months after Dad died, on sixteenth January 2004, Nick and I wed in Caldicot Castle, a beautiful place. The day was magical, but it was so sad that Dad wasn't there. He would go on and on about coming to our wedding, and I couldn't burst his bubble but I knew he wouldn't have made it. He would have been so happy. He thought highly of Nick and would often say to him, 'She's hard work, but she's worth it.' How rude!

One of our bridesmaids was Zoë, another of the children from the *Born To Be Different* series. After the first series was shown on TV, her mum, Annmarie, and I started writing to each other (back in the day when good old pen and paper was enough!). We met again at the first *Born To Be Different* party and stayed good friends ever since.

Shelbie, of course, found the whole day hugely boring and pretty much slept through it all, but she did look darned cute in her little bridesmaid dress. Not that she agreed; she made no exception for it being my wedding and before the day was out, she managed to poop all over the dress as she did whenever I put a dress on her. She was a tomboy through and through and hated dresses. Why I thought this day would be any different I really don't know!

For Dad's Day (A Poem I Wrote for Dad's Funeral)

I've sat here trying to write this for you,
But, Dad, the words won't come.
How do you say about all the great things in a few words
When you feel so numb?

As I'm sat in the garden it's starting to rain
So I look up to the heavens above,
And I wonder how we'll ever accept that you're gone
That we can't feel your love.

The many times I've written these words
Being positive and trying to be strong
But we feel we can't lie when we don't feel like that
So that's why the words come out wrong.

So from my heart I write this for you,
It's our hearts that are breaking right now
And we can't stop this pain, whatever we do
We could try, but we just don't know how.

But Dad is the one who makes it all right,
Dad is the one who knows how
And when it's your dad that had to go
We have to do it alone right now.

We love you Dad, we always will
We'll remember your eyes and your smile,
We know that no one can break this bond
No matter the distance or mile.

Time to go and get on with our day
But every step there'll be you,
Maybe we won't see it for quite some time
But you're there, your love shining through.

Thank you, Dad for being you,
We're proud to be blessed for so long.
You showed us so much, you taught us to love
So for you we'll try to be strong.

Chapter Four

About two years after Shelbie's ptosis surgery, she started using her eyes. Up until this point she was still feeling her way around and using her ears to "see". If I put a toy on the floor she would listen to where I'd put it and feel around in that area until she found it. Especially her keys. Someone had bought her a set of toy keys for her third Christmas. These were her absolute favourite and remained so for over ten years. When I put the keys on the floor with other toys she would go straight for them, picking the other toys up and discarding them until she felt what she was looking for. But she'd never actually attempted to look for them. Now we were noticing that she seemed to be directly looking at or looking for things. She would look at it, then turn away and feel for it, but it was a huge breakthrough that she was looking first.

Then she then started making eye contact and looking at everything. In fact, she became very nosey! She was also good at making choices and when she was younger, for a long time she loved *Tweenies* and *Fimbles* — but *Tweenies* more! If you got two or three DVDs and asked her to pick one more often than not it was *Tweenies*. We even used to switch them around to confuse her, but she would still go for the same one. It was a definite choice and this was a big thing for us.

On meeting her for the first time you could be fooled into believing she was this sweet, poorly little girl who didn't have much quality of life but, believe me, how wrong you would be! There was a lot going on in that little girl's head and she knew how to use it to her advantage. She was actually very smart and could speak volumes without using any words.

With all of my children, from a small age I would stand them on my feet to walk around, guessing it would probably help teach them to walk by giving them that sense of walking. It was no different with Shelbs. Nick and I did the same with her. When she was about five, she dragged a foot towards herself. We thought it might be coincidence or luck or something, but no, she did it again and again, gaining more steps, and if you sat her sideways on your lap, put a hand on her bottom and on her stomach and said, 'Stand up, Shelbie,' she would straighten her legs and stand on command. We started hoping, believing even, that one day, with aid, she might actually walk. But she had a big fit many months later, requiring ventilation and an overnight stay in PICU, and when we took her home the following day she wouldn't even roll. She just lay there. She couldn't move her right side at all and we weren't sure if this would be permanent. Supposing the fit had done too much damage? Thankfully, weeks later she gained the use of her right side again as if nothing had happened. But as for her standing and walking? She seemed to have lost that forever. This was one huge punch in the stomach. Why were we spending all this time learning so much for it to cruelly be taken away again? A lot of what she did seemed bittersweet at times, but I was still so, so proud of her when she did achieve these things. And she was still very naughty, which I always found comical, so it wasn't all bad. It's just that these blips knock you sideways at times.

Shelbie had a very infectious smile — as I mentioned, she might have got this from Dad — and this is something that from start to end she never lost. She had quite a wicked sense of humour. If someone was being told off or they had hurt themselves, you could guarantee she would find this amusing. If we were out shopping and you heard a baby crying all of a sudden you would hear this little chuckle. She was also such a rebel. She used to kick things — never hurting herself, but kicking them until they broke. It didn't matter how many times you moved her away she would roll back until she had done the damage she'd set out to do. It was like a magnetic force: she just had to go back to it. She broke our fireplace, the TV unit... the list grew ever longer. They even said in school that everything on the walls that was Shelbie's height when she's rolling had been trashed. We walked in the class one day and at first glance all the displays looked lovely until you looked lower down and Margarita, who was her teacher at the time (and who would go on to become a great friend), pointed out that anything in Shelbie's reach had been kicked, ripped and/or smashed.

If I was telling someone about something naughty she'd done — like in school when the children were playing with bowls of water and she picked her bowl up and lobbed it across the classroom, or when I was baking at home and she'd managed to get the bag of flour and throw it with a huge grin — as I told the story she would start laughing. She understood everything you were saying.

But Shelbs was horrendous for sleeping at night, in spite of different medication. The lack of sleep seemed to start when she began going to school. It was like a light had been switched on and she decided life was too short to sleep. Sleeping was for wimps and, despite sometimes making herself ill from it, she just couldn't give in. She would shout and shout until you went into her, and when you finally gave in and, tired and weary-eyed and not in the best of moods, dragged yourself into her room, she would be there with her nasal cannulas in her mouth, blowing raspberries against the oxygen that was meant to be delivered to her, the tape we'd used to keep the prongs in place to deliver the O_2 pulling her eyes down. At the thought that someone had come in to play with her she'd offer a huge smile and be clapping with her hands and feet in excitement. That would just melt your heart as she looked so cute and so funny, and she would fold her arms as if to say, 'Thank you, got my own way.'

Shelbie had a major fit when she was about four years old. A doctor who had never met her before asked if we should consider "letting her go". I was fuming. She had only had a fit and he was basically telling us that we were being unfair, doing this to her all the time. At this point she was actually rarely in hospital and certainly not in PICU very often which meant more times than not she was well, and while it was that way, she had a better quality of life. I told him that when it started being the other way around, we would consider it, but that would be done in consultation with Huw Thomas or Dr Stanley — the doctors that knew her — not some jumped up nobody who'd never met my child before and assumed that her life was unfair. What ignorance! While I appreciate they only see these children at their worst, he should have come round to our house and seen her up to her antics, planning her next bout of mayhem. You could see it in her eyes when she'd got mischief on her mind, and that was a quality of life that you could never let her miss out on. How could we let her go and stop her enjoying life so much?

Shelbie did love life and lived it to the max when she was well. Her quality of life could be immense. In fact, even when she was ill, she still tried being happy. There's no way would I have ever let her stop having that. Many people who haven't half the battles don't appreciate what's in front of them, while she just lived a new day each day as if she was grateful God has graced her with another one. That's an amazing feeling and something I wouldn't have experienced if God hadn't chosen me to look after her. How privileged was I!

Despite us being told Shelbie would always be on oxygen, she wanted to try without. The choice was literally hers and, as she kept pulling her nasal prongs completely off her face, I thought, 'OK, we'll give it a go; she needs to have a say in things as well.' She was, of course, absolutely correct because she was managing without it most of the time. She sometimes needed it at night or if she was ill, but otherwise could do amazingly without it. She very much knew her own mind.

When she was five and a half, she became a big sister to Kalan, who was born in April 2005. She wasn't a lover of babies as a rule and enjoyed hitting out at them. It was a sort of cause and effect, she hits it, it makes a noise. It seemed to give her immense satisfaction, like working out the instructions of a toy. The following December she went into hospital with a chest infection. She had pseudomonas, which is a bacterium that lays dormant until Shelbs became ill when it reared its ugly head tenfold. Shelbie kept deteriorating and a doctor I'd met years before (when Jane's son was dying) told me he was very concerned about Shelbie. He said we weren't off to PICU yet, but he had briefed them already.

Thankfully, she didn't end up in PICU this time, but she had a very lengthy stay in hospital and the staff kept threatening to start charging us rent. I even spent my thirtieth birthday in there with her. Yippee! Who needs a big hall in which to celebrate a Big Day when you have a whole children's ward? It didn't matter where we were; we were all together and that's what mattered. Shelbie quite enjoyed the pink champagne. She was a bit of a rebel when it came to alcohol. She loved beer but her favourite was Guinness and, no, I didn't wait until she was eighteen for her to drink alcohol. That would have been very presumptuous, assuming that she would still be with us by then, and so we were cramming everything in for her to try as quickly as we could. (I drew the line at smoking though: with chronic lung disease I didn't think the two would go well together!)

After a few months we were going in the right direction of going home. One morning the doctor came in while I was sat painting with Kalan, and informed us we could leave. Shelbie had been on the floor with me, Kalan and Aunty Emma painting, but as I lifted her onto her bed to get her ready to escape, I noticed that she felt very hot all of a sudden. We took her temperature and she was indeed hot. She was 39°C. As she is a hypothermic child her normal range runs between 34°C and 35°C. Great, I thought, we're going nowhere.

I changed her pad and noticed she had a rash on her tummy. I called the doctor back and asked her if she thought it looked like chicken pox. She felt it did, so marked the spots, observed Shelbie for a few hours and as there were more it was decided she would stay in overnight to see how things went. By the following day she was really unwell and started having desaturations in her O_2 levels so she ended up staying in hospital until the chicken pox went. But it wasn't all doom and gloom in the hospital. Infection control, of course, were having kittens. Shelbs had been in contact with no one who was ill from our family, nor any staff as far as they could ascertain. She was always in isolation as she was MRSA positive, so for the last two months when she'd been in hospital, her contact with other people had been limited. No one else on the ward or who had been around Shelbie showed any symptoms, so it made no sense really. But it did make us chuckle, because they were expecting an outbreak but no, little Shelbs just had it to herself. The nurses kept saying to Infection control, 'Oh, that's just Shelbs for you.' But I don't think they were all that happy. In the end they had to admit defeat, and never did work out how she caught it.

Finally, she came home from hospital and life got back to our normal. Kalan was ten months old and was already learning what life was like growing up in and around hospital. He had fallen off the bed while we were there, learned to walk there, and his first experience of "normal" was when he was just five days old and Shelbs had her first ever asthma attack — a new one to write in her book of diagnostic achievements! As such, hospital really was home from home for him as much as it was for Shelbs and the others, but he was a lot more accepting of it, maybe because he was born into it but also because we'd learned about keeping the children with us so he didn't care where he was as long as we were together.

Any child's first years are precious, but when we think of how poorly Shelbie had been at times, and knowing her life was limited, we valued our days with our children even more.

In June 2006, we had another baby boy when Mackenzie joined the family. With four boys and two girls we felt very fortunate and very blessed. Around this time the Woodlands Unit at Southmead closed down, and so now all of Shelbie's care would be at Bristol Children's Hospital. This was a very difficult change for us all, to say the least. Shelbie accepted it, but I struggled for a long time. She had been in a little ward, where she was well known and kind of top dog. Now she would just be a little fish in a big sea and it scared me. It didn't seem so personal, and I worried that they wouldn't be able to give her the kind of care and attention she had had before and so very much needed. I guess only time would tell. One blessing, though, was she would still have some of her old nurses around her, as well as her beloved Dr Thomas and Dr Stanley.

This Beauty

Have you ever stopped and thought
About the wonders we see each day?
There's beauty all around us
We rush by, let it pass our way.

Stop for a minute, breathe it all in
Take some time to acknowledge it all.
The sky, the ground, the leaves on the tree
In the autumn, the beauty when they fall

The cold crispy nights as Christmas draws near,
The memories of snow falling down,
The one season families make time for each other
When there's laughter — what a great sound

It's over too quickly, another year's gone by
Another time we've just expected it to be
What if this was taken from us?
What do you think we'd see?

I thank God for all He has given
My family so precious to me
We're blessed with the beauty of our lives
So just stop and take in what you see.

Chapter Five

Life was happily manic with six children to look after. The first year of Mackenzie's life flew by, as had Kalan's. Where Kalan was a very active baby, however, and had been from day one, Mac was the complete opposite. He was so laid back and appeared in no rush to learn anything or do anything. He just sat and watched Kalan buzzing around. But they were both very happy babies.

Shelbie had been doing well since her last illness, although, just after Mac reached his first birthday in the summer of 2007 when she was about seven and a half years old, she had diarrhoea. Nothing unusual there, but she ended up in hospital with dehydration. No bugs were found, then it seemed to clear up. This happened again a few times, no sooner was she over one bout when she had it back again. We spoke to the dietician who tried changing Shelbie's feeds, but to no avail. I started taking her more and more regularly to hospital, saying that something wasn't right.

It was Huw Thomas who listened to what I had to say. In Huw I'd found an ally, a doctor who listens. In my experience they are few and far between, but they do exist. He took bloods tests, stool samples, urine, everything you could think of. He was always so thorough, but, unfortunately, we got no answers.

Shelbie started deteriorating in herself. I felt we were losing her, but just couldn't work out why. There seemed to be nothing behind her eyes, it was as if the spark was gone, and she wasn't enjoying life. She had little moments — sporadic — where she would clap and smile but it never seemed heartfelt, more like she was doing it for us. We stopped going out much because every time we did, we would end up with a pool of faeces either in her wheelchair or, worse, all over the floor where it had dripped through her chair. It didn't matter how often we changed her she would leak immediately and, considering she was a child who had always suffered constipation, this was far from normal for her. We even went over the allocated amount of continence pads we were given per delivery and had to beg, borrow and steal just to ensure she was never left in a dirty pad.

Nick and I were going away for an anniversary weekend. My brother, Paul, and his wife, Emma, were having the children and a friend who was also a nurse was going to look after Shelbs but at the last minute that fell through so we took her with us which, to be fair, was nothing unusual. If Nick and I had the rare occasion of no children, you could guarantee that didn't include Shelbie. There she would be, every time, right in the middle of us. We went to the Isle of Wight, and it was beautiful. We decided that the first day would be for Madam and on the second we would do what we wanted to do. So, that first day took us to see the Waltzing Waters in Ryde, which Shelbs thoroughly enjoyed, and the following day we decided to walk around the shops then go to a pub for a bit of lunch as Shelbie could roll around the floor while we ate. First stop was a toy shop to get Shelbie something to play with to keep her happy while we ambled around, as she used to get bored quite easily. As I was standing at the cash desk paying for the toy, I looked around and could see poo dripping onto the floor under her chair. I couldn't believe it. (Mind you, it's funny how she waited until I'd paid for the toy!) There was such a mess by the time we got back to the car. We cleared up what we could and made sure Shelbie was clean but then had to head straight back to where we were staying to bath her and scrub down her wheelchair. We couldn't be bothered to go out after that — and we had to wait for her chair to dry anyway — so we got food in and watched a film, sitting on the floor with her rolling around beside us. Thanks, Shelbs, for your part in such a fantastic, romantic, anniversary weekend!

In all seriousness, though, what you might call "normal" life was just becoming impossible. I dreaded going out, so it became easier not to. This went on for six months and became what felt like an endless battle as, each time Shelbie was admitted to hospital, doctors would send her home twenty-four hours later saying there was nothing wrong. Finally, one day, after I had had a breakdown in the hospital with a lot of colourful language after they'd sent us home yet again and we'd reappeared the following day, Dr Stanley told me and all the other doctors that Shelbie was not to go home until we had, in his words, 'Got to the bottom of this.'

'Excuse the pun,' he added, a joke that would be made many times after.

The weeks went on and more tests and endless scans came and went but we were no closer to discovering the problem and Shelbie was getting drastically worse. It was coming up to Christmas and Shelbs started drifting in and out of consciousness. The doctor looking after her over the Christmas period was Doug Heller. What a guy! I think he was the most dedicated doctor I ever came across in all the hospital days. He would be honest, he would listen, he would specifically ask Nick how he was feeling and how he was managing with work. As a rule — certainly in my experience — women are quite lucky as friends will ask the difficult questions about emotions and feelings, and generally as women, to a degree, we can be open about how we feel. But men, I find, don't always tend to have it as easy. It was such a relief that a man could ask another man how he was doing and seem genuinely interested in the reply.

He also started to get frustrated himself, though. 'I'm a doctor,' he said to us one day. 'I'm meant to make people better, but I cannot work out what is wrong with Shelbie.' He was showing he was human, and we needed that.

Nick had suggested to several doctors and every surgeon we came across over the weeks about doing a CT scan, as it would be more detailed than a normal abdominal scan and, hopefully, they could work out from there what was going on. But no one was interested, they kept trying to convince us that if there was anything the other scans would have already picked it up.

On Christmas Eve, Mum, Paul and Emma came in to open presents with Shelbie. She was still drifting in and out of consciousness, but mainly out, and not really aware of the presents or even the visitors. The following day we let the children bring in a load of presents that they had opened at home and we brought Shelbie's presents too, but she didn't wake up. She was completely out of it, so we didn't open any. We told her they would be waiting for her at home when she got better, but to be honest I never thought she was ever going to open them.

Just days after Christmas, Dr Heller took us out of Shelbs' room and said, 'I'm really concerned, your little girl is very poorly.' I asked if we needed to call family in and he nodded.

As I was walking off the ward, a nurse we had known since Shelbie was a baby asked if I was OK. I said, 'We're losing her, aren't we?' She said that things didn't look good and I knew then that this was probably it. She agreed with Dr Heller that it was a good idea to contact my family.

I went outside, built up my strength with a few cigarettes and rang my mum first. She was away at the time. Then I called my brothers and told them all through heartache and tears that if they wanted to see Shelbie, they'd better make it sooner rather than later as I couldn't see her pulling through this one.

Then I realised I hadn't told my dearest friend that Shelbie was even ill. Margarita was in Cyprus visiting her family and I hadn't wanted to ruin that so I'd decided not to tell her. I realised now that she needed to know. We had been friends for a good few years, and she had often been my rock and also had the most incredible connection with Shelbie. She had started as her teacher in school and Shelbie absolutely idolised her. She understood Shelbie better than most and was like a surrogate mum to her. I called her, and then headed back to the ward.

Nick was still persisting about a CT scan. Shelbie by this point was having daily scans of her stomach as we were convinced the problem was there. Her body had started swelling; we had to change her feeding button to two sizes larger because of this. Her protein and albumin were low which was making fluids leak throughout her body in all the wrong places. Her breathing was highly compromised, and we had to keep her sat up to help with her breathing, but she wasn't tolerating that either. Despite being barely conscious, she would continuously push herself back down the bed. She hated sitting but didn't understand the necessity behind it. It did make us giggle though, that with all she was going through she was still objecting to sitting. I mean, really! Shelbie was always, 'I'll do it if I want and when I want,' which showed that she still had some fight in her.

Dr Heller came in during the early hours sometimes to check on Shelbie, even all over Christmas. Nick started badgering him about the CT again, reasoning that even if it showed nothing, for the sake of a test and to shut the parents up why couldn't they just do it. 'At least if she does die, we can say we tried everything.' Dr Heller agreed it sounded plausible and started supporting us in pushing for it and, just over a week after Christmas, the CT scan was scheduled — despite us being warned that they weren't expecting to find anything. Yada-yada-ya. I didn't care. At least she was getting it.

Dr Heller came down with us for the scan, and while we were waiting, Shelbie opened her eyes for the first time in over a week. Nick and I were so excited. Dr Heller much less so. With a chuckle I said, 'This is probably the one time you don't want her awake and moving,' and he nodded, looking rather displeased. Oh, that was so truly Shelbie. "Trust Shelbs," as we often said. In fact, though, she was actually very good for the scan. Nick went in with her, while I sat in the waiting room crying. Worry, exhaustion, maybe even a bit of relief, I don't know, but it was hard.

We went back to the ward and a while later the doctors came in. Their words blew me away. 'We can't believe it, but we've found a perforation in Shelbie's bowel. She needs an operation as soon as possible.'

They were going to operate that night, but an emergency came in so Miss McNally, who was going to operate, moved Shelbie back to the following day. She came in with the consent forms and explained the risks. Shelbie was very sick so the risk was high, but she would die without the operation anyway. When I looked at the consent form and it said in black and white, "risk of mortality" I lost it. I just broke down and couldn't sign what was potentially my daughter's death warrant. And I was angry, too. If the CT had been done three weeks earlier when Nick had first started asking for it, she wouldn't be so weak and unstable now. In the end, Nick signed the form as I just couldn't cope with much more. Matt and Laura came to the hospital in the evening for moral support, and we snuck in some beers and had a few drinks and even managed a few laughs. It was a good distraction and took that nauseous feeling away a little bit. For a while, at least.

The following morning, Mr Rogers introduced himself, saying he would now be doing the surgery. Can you imagine the discussion in the staff room trying to decide who would do it? Talk about drawing the short straw, he really must have drawn the shortest straw they could find. He was a very gentle man, and quietly spoken. Shelbs' operation was scheduled for half past two that afternoon, so we had the morning with her at least. We had no visitors that day, as we just wanted to spend what little time we had left with her. Thankfully, Paul and Emma had moved into our house temporarily to look after the children, so we could be with Shelbs any time day or night which was good because we'd had a couple of early morning calls when she was deteriorating.

The morning seemed to drag but at the same time flew by. At one thirty the nurse came in and said they were ready for her. I was so upset. I felt I had been cheated out of a whole hour with her. It's heart-wrenching every time you have to take a child to theatre but this was so much more intense. For starters, Shelbie would normally be bouncing around on the way down but she wasn't even conscious this time and she was so, so weak. All we could do now was wait.

We sat in Shelbie's room looking out onto the ward. Every time a nurse walked past, we thought she was coming in to tell us Shelbs hadn't made it. Every time the phone rang, I'd watch the nurse's face to see if she looked upset or worried, to see if they had rung to say, 'Shelbs is no longer with us.' We sat for hours, but it felt like days. I had only prayer and God's love as security — I often don't realise it, but that's all you need. Six months before all this had happened, I'd realised that there was something missing big time, despite having a wonderful life, and I knew instantly what it was. I started going back to the church I had attended throughout my childhood, well, as much as Shelbie's illness would allow me to attend anyway. I asked God for forgiveness and to come back into my life and I continued to attend until we'd seemingly become permanent residents at the hospital. He came to reach for me at a perfect time because without Him walking by my side in this "hell road" I would have fallen time and again and not been able to get up. I'd drifted years before but I knew He would accept me back with open arms and no questions asked. I felt Him by my side when I needed Him most — and this really was the time I needed Him most!

After four hours, our nurse walked through the door. I felt sick. She told us they'd taken Shelbie to intensive care. 'They will call us when they have stabilised her.'

I burst into tears. 'She's alive?'

'Yes,' she smiled.

Matt and Laura were with us, and we went to get fresh air and coffee while we waited to go to see Shelbie. There were people from the *Born To Be Different* film crew waiting in reception. I ran down shouting, 'She's alive, she's alive.'

Three hours later — and after a much-needed kebab! — we were called to PICU. Matt and Laura waited in the parents' room while we went in to see her. We knew her nurse, Rachel, as she had cared for her at home as well. She was very open with us and said that Shelbie was very, very weak. 'I know,' I replied, 'but she is alive, and none of you thought she would be.' We thought lunchtime was the last time we were ever going to see her. Rachel repeated just how weak and poorly she was. The doctor had explained that they'd needed to remove half of Shelbie's bowel and she now had a colostomy bag. I didn't care. She was alive, and that's all that mattered. Matt and Laura came in and Rachel suggested putting us up in the hospital, but I couldn't bring myself to do it. The last time I'd stayed in the hospital my child had died and I never really got over that. So, we stayed in a hotel just two minutes down the road.

The coming weeks were very tough and seemed to be characterised by the fact that every time we got somewhere there would be a setback, like when Shelbie managed to get E. coli in her lungs, for example. Things started really going backwards. They found pus collections at the front of her stomach before her operation and a week or so into her PICU stay they feared she had more collections. They put a drain in her left side, but that made no difference as nothing drained out. Meanwhile, as her albumin had been low, her stitches weren't healing properly and so her scar was constantly leaking.

Our PICU doctor, David Grant, came in to talk to us. He said that she couldn't be left with these collections, but she would probably die being moved to have the CT. So, she'd die if we moved her, or die if we didn't. They were waiting for the surgical team to make a decision. The following day was a Saturday and we had the chaplain from the children's hospice we use come to visit us. Chris, the doctor on that weekend, asked to talk to us. 'Look,' he started, 'we are really concerned.

One dose of the drugs Shelbie is on would clear a chest infection in an adult. Shelbie is receiving it regularly and not responding. She is that unstable, if we stopped any of her heart drugs now, she would just die straight away.' We counted how many syringe drivers she had administering drugs: twelve. And that was on top of the regular medication she was on. Her heart was never usually a problem on a day-to-day basis, but it was suffering now, and every time they turned her, she would become bradycardic — her heart rate dropped.

I sobbed. 'Please don't give up on her, don't ask me to let her go.'

'I'm not,' Chris assured me. 'I'm just saying we've done all we can. Now it is down to her.'

Shelbie was stubborn and clever, but she was so weak at this point. Could she really turn this around this time? I just prayed and prayed that God would heal her on this earth but knew that His healing could very well mean promoting her to Heaven. People can often get confused and think that someone isn't healed if they don't get better and survive. Yet sometimes they are healed so they can be completely out of pain, but just not on this earth.

Chris told us after PICU that he was dreading that weekend with us because he thought she was going to die on his watch. Her numbers from her blood gases where they check things like lactate, acid, protein, sodium, CRP, CO_2, pH levels etc. were all so bad the following morning. By Saturday teatime we hardly dared to believe that some of the numbers were improving. We were told surgeons would make a decision soon and a few days later we were driving into hospital about seven in the morning and I had had enough. I felt sick going in, not knowing what the day would hold. I had already had a meltdown at home before I left, and I just broke down to God and said, 'Lord, I need a sign either way, I just can't carry on another day not knowing.' And as I finished that prayer that very second a song came on the radio and I heard the words:

People keep talking, they can say what they like, all I know is everything's gonna be alright. No one can get in the way of what I'm feeling.

I responded with a, 'Thank you!' and actually dared to walk into PICU without having a panic attack — something on previous mornings I couldn't do. I would send Nick in first to see how bad she was, then he would come back to the parents' room to get me and prepare me one way or the other. We walked into her cubicle and the surgeons said they felt it was just fluid in the collections which would settle on its own, so there was no need for more surgery.

Her stomach had swollen again and her stitches were splitting, but this all just started to calm down. Shelbs continued to get better and stronger each day and after a month in PICU she headed back to the ward. It wasn't easy as she wasn't tolerating food, whatever we tried. Miss Cusick, her general surgeon, suggested that if she tolerated none of the feeds, we would need to look into TPN — intravenous feeds. This would entail months of training and a lot more work at home. But we would do it, we were just eager to get home. In addition, Shelbie would need a portacath inserted for constant IV access which Miss Cusick wasn't comfortable about, due to Shelbie always being MRSA positive. It would certainly put her at more risk of infections. And then, of course, there was always the risk of her becoming septic as had happened in the past when infections managed to get into her bloodstream. Luckily, a feed was found that worked. It was an elemental feed — a feed that contains some nutrients such as protein and fat that are broken down already to make digestion easier. Shelbie was also suffering withdrawal from the PICU meds. She was on anti-withdrawal drugs but seemed to still suffer slightly. She would have involuntary movements, discomfort and distress and a glazy look as if she wasn't truly there. No smiles as yet, I noticed.

I was chatting to my brother, Matt, and realised I had put a lot of pressure on her. I had said to her on one of the tough days in PICU, 'You don't have permission to go anywhere. If you keep fighting to the end, I'll fight with you every step of the way.' I asked Matt, 'What if she wanted to go, and I bullied her into fighting?'

He simply replied, 'What if she felt she couldn't do it and was about to give up, then you said that to her which made her fight on, knowing you believed in her?'

He was right, but when she was just sitting there with no smiles I wondered, 'What have I done? Have I pushed her too far?'

Finally, in March, and after nearly four months in hospital, Shelbie was ready for discharge. We took her home to the Christmas tree and decorations, and all her presents were waiting on her bed. We had a family Christmas dinner with crackers and all the trimmings. I remember time after time sitting on that bed, wondering whether she would ever open her presents or ever sleep in this room again. I thought how quiet it was in there, and that it could be forever like that if she didn't make it home. But here she was once more. We had promised her Christmas when she was well enough, and we kept that promise. We were slowly getting our old Shelbs back, with smiles and kisses, and she loved all her presents. As time went on and we saw more and more of her cheekiness, we knew we had made the right decision. And however hard this is to swallow for some, God had His hand in that situation the whole way through. If we can't be tested as Christians, then how will we know how dedicated we are?

Just after Shelbie went back to the ward, we had found out we were expecting again. I was happy as I always am with a new life, but I couldn't even think about enjoying the pregnancy until Shelbie was safely home. People kept telling me that I had to look after myself, I'd got a baby to consider and so on. But I had a child here and now who needed me, and this baby would have to be robust to last in our house anyway, so start as you mean to go on! It may be hard for some to grasp that attitude, but I knew my little girl and I didn't know this new life yet so Shelbie took priority. She had my time and energy, and the baby got fed and had whatever energy I had left, and that was how it had to be. Before I was pregnant, I told Shelbs I would fight the fight with her — for her, if needed — and I wasn't breaking my promise.

Once she came home, I booked myself in at the antenatal clinic. I was already twenty weeks pregnant. They weren't impressed with me but I knew the baby was OK. I could feel her kicking and now, with my family back together again, I could really enjoy my pregnancy.

Kalan started nursery once Shelbs came home and I met some fantastic friends there. There was a little group of us — Leah, Terri, Mel, Sarah and Katie — and not only did we have a good laugh but they were all very supportive. Unfortunately, I don't see any of them nowadays aside from Leah as life takes over with jobs and everything, but Leah has stayed my rock and had a fantastic relationship with Shelbie. She rough and tumbled Shelbie, which she always likes, and Shelbie would kick Leah as hard as she could with her little boots and find it all very amusing.

In September 2008, Shelbie finally went back to school after a year off. The following month we had a little girl, Cienna, to welcome into our family. With the usual chaos around family life, we couldn't arrange any respite so Shelbie was at the birth. She felt very special about it, although she fell asleep at the crucial moment and woke seconds after it was over. Very well timed! Shelbie was buzzing in school the following day, though, and life was once again our normal.

Smile

Having a child with special needs — what's it like?
I get asked so often — 'How do you cope?'
It does feel like a thankless job sometimes — you think you're not gonna
win...

Then they smile—
It happened a long time after you expected it to,
But that's what makes each and every smile
So much more special.

You go from day to day with the same routine:
You wake up and it's feeding, drugs,
Physio, stimulation, appointments—
Some of it heart-wrenching...
Again comes that's smile.

Toward the end of the day you're ready to collapse, all energy gone.
Ready to quit yet again and say, 'That's it I've had enough...'
Again — comes that smile,
So you can go a little further.

Things so trivial, at the time seem so important, then you realise:
I don't want to be thanked, it's because of love I do this.
I don't care about tomorrow—
What I have now is today.
And not to be told you're loved back doesn't matter—
Because I know what I have...
That smile—
That one expression that's changed my world—
That beautiful, beautiful smile.

Chapter Six

In February 2009 I took Shelbie (now still only nine) into hospital because she wasn't tolerating her food again, a situation that had been going on for some months. We spoke to Miss Cusick who explained that she couldn't do anything surgically as Shelbie's stomach was so fragile, and in such a mess after her bowel surgery. The year before she had started getting more collections, mainly between the liver and pancreas, so had needed intravenous antibiotics. These collections just kept appearing, and things would settle again a while later. I think that after so much going on with her stomach and then these collections as well, it had just about given up. Her body had been put under so much stress something was going to break. She had total gut dysmotility — her stomach was failing to work. But at least we now knew what the problem was.

In order to find out what was going on, Shelbie had been admitted once more. While she was in, Dr Thomas, who generally oversaw all her care, was getting her ready for discharge — dotting the Is and crossing the Ts — when he noticed that quite a few of her routine blood sugars seemed very high. He wasn't overly concerned but wanted to eliminate diabetes and suchlike.

About six months before this admission, I'd taken Shelbs into the emergency department (ED for short) because she was dehydrated and there seemed to be no cause for it. The doctors weren't concerned and sent us home but it kept happening, she would look very dry so I would give her additional fluids, yet her pads were constantly saturated. Every time I took her back the doctors would point out that her pads would be soaked because I'd increased her fluids, whereas my argument was that I was giving her more because she was dry, and if she's dry, her body would absorb the extra fluid and not wee it straight back out. So, if she is urinating more, it's because her body doesn't need it, and if her body didn't need it, she would be hydrated, not dehydrated. But they didn't get it. They couldn't seem to understand what I was saying and I — once again — was going round in circles. It felt like they were treating me as if I was finding a problem that wasn't there. I didn't like being in that place anyway so I wouldn't take her unless it was absolutely necessary. I was usually right in the past when I knew something was wrong, but unfortunately in my experience doctors still aren't good enough at listening to parents' expertise when it comes to knowing their own children. (I'll admit that there are parents out there who almost certainly waste doctors' time by taking their children to the GP just for a runny nose or whatever, but there are many more parents who need to be listened to.) And when you are a regular and are known to the doctors, they should know better than to dismiss you. After many years training they will still never know a child like a parent does.

Consequently, Dr Thomas arranged for a blood glucose test to be done. They put a high amount of glucose into Shelbie to see what her blood sugar levels would be. If she hadn't got diabetes, her body would tolerate it without it causing her blood sugars to rise too high, but it did rise, very high, showing that Shelbie had diabetes. OK, well I guess we're not going home soon then…

We were introduced to Dr Bragonier, our endocrine consultant for Shelbie's diabetes. I realised this was the doctor on duty the weekend Jane's son had died, so we had already met a few times before, which was nice. I always did struggle when we had to get to know new doctors. We were also introduced to our diabetes nurse, Helen. Both were very supportive and trained us to deal with the condition. This was all the more confusing because Shelbie was tube fed and couldn't talk, but it was all doable. We just had to learn little ways with her that would indicate if her bloods were too high or too low.

After this diagnosis, and learning that Shelbie's gut had given up, she was eventually fitted with a gastrojejunostomy feeding tube, so she would be fed straight into the jejunum — part of the bowel — and thus bypass the stomach altogether. She had two ports: one for the bowel and another for the stomach for the delivery of medication. The food had to be fed through very slowly so Shelbie was on what they class as continuous feeds, but we did manage to have six hours a day off. Shelbie didn't tolerate the drugs into her stomach, though, so those too had to be administered via the jejunum, and it all took a very long time. The drugs had to be delivered at the rate of a millilitre every two minutes. As Shelbie was on about fifty drugs altogether, her regular four-times-a-day medication routine took up a very long time.

We expected we would go home about a week after surgery, once they knew the new tube was working well, but Shelbie as usual had other plans. She pulled the whole tube out from her bowel and ended up having an internal bleed which required a blood transfusion. OK, so now we can wait a few days for her to settle after the transfusion and then look into going home, right? Wrong. Shelbie's condition started to deteriorate, and she developed septicaemia so needed strong intravenous drugs. Thankfully, they kicked in pretty quickly, but then Dr Thomas came into her room with a serious expression and a sentence starting with, 'Now...'

Surely there couldn't be anything else? But there was. They'd discovered that Shelbie had tubulopathy — leaky kidneys, to you and me. She was started on four new drugs for that, and we told Dr Thomas that if Shelbie didn't love him so much, he would be banned! But a doctor good at his job and finding things wrong with my child made life so much easier for us. And she loved him so much we called him Uncle Huw when we would talk to Shelbie about him — or even in front of him — and she knew who it was and would give a huge grin. Even as a baby she would settle at the sound of his voice, which was very comforting when I couldn't be there with her.

We finally got home after a month of many new diagnoses. After Shelbie had come out of PICU last time, I felt I needed to be attending church, so I found one local to us rather than travelling to the church I'd grown up in. I'm not the best with timekeeping as it is, and this gave me more of a chance to, well, I wouldn't say be on time, but to be less late! It was a warm and welcoming church, the pastor was gifted when speaking and his wife was a lovely singer with an even lovelier heart. It was going well, and at times I also attended Paul and Emma's church, but after a while, things started feeling hard, like I was being pulled down, and I didn't know why. There seemed to be this hold on me, spiritually, that is, and I couldn't shake it. Sometimes I think life just gets in the way, the stresses and tiredness of it, and at other times it's the devil that gets in the way. I loved what I did, I felt important being a mother and especially honoured being Shelbs' mum, but at times it's bloody hard and, although you may have a hundred people around you, you can still feel alone. I think tiredness just got the better of me sometimes and this may have been what I had been going through.

Shelbie, of course, continued to do things her way, as her sense of mischievousness continued unabated. While she was in hospital in the summer of 2009 — so she would have been coming on for ten years old — she was adamant she wasn't going to give up any blood. The doctor had tried a few times, but our rule was that you get three attempts and then you leave her be, as trying to take bloods always upset her. We introduced this to our regime after a commotion in hospital just after her little friend's funeral. The doctor just kept stabbing her and stabbing her to get bloods. I kicked off a bit and she made my friend, Jane, take me off the ward. Shelbs had at least thirteen pinpricks in her from where the doctor had attempted, unsuccessfully, to take some blood. Had they acted hours earlier when I had first asked, Shelbs would have been slightly easier to bleed and not as distressed. At the time I was fearful the doctor would get security to remove me, but as I became more confident over time, I began to make things clearer to the doctors as to what we would — and what we would not — tolerate, and this new rule regarding three strikes to get blood was one of the things we brought in.

So now this poor doctor had had his three tries. He was new, and I'm sure Shelbie knew who the newbies were and thought she would have fun and games with him. He wasn't sure what else to do as we really needed these bloods. I asked him, 'Why don't you pinprick her toes or fingers like you would to check her BM or HbA1c?' He explained that a capillary (venous) blood test goes straight into the syringe without any air getting in, whereas a finger prick blood test lets air in and often the numbers come back higher. Not by much, but enough to change the result (although nowadays a lot more doctors are using finger prick tests as they've realised that, being honest, there isn't actually a great deal of difference). I suggested that while I understood what he was saying, why didn't he try it that way anyway, and then, for example, if you know that the result goes up by two you can just knock two off the outcome. It would be better than nothing, and at least we'd all have a general idea of where she was at.

He actually said that it made sense and agreed to do try it.

Shelbie usually bled well for us when we did it at home and I just suggested he use a sharper needle, but this was Shelbie and this time she decided to give her blood sparingly. It took ages. It was dripping out, painfully slowly, and meanwhile she was laughing the whole way through; finger prick testing never bothered her in the slightest. Then she whacked the bottle and spilt the precious little bit we had. The poor doctor started sweating, and I'm not sure my laughter helped at all. I did try telling her off, but she just laughed at me and followed this up with a raspberry. And, as if things couldn't get any worse, Shelbs reached forwards and grabbed his glasses, pulling them off and throwing them across the room. Poor guy, he was so lovely as well! When she wanted, Shelbs could be so horrid at times, but always with that mischievous smile and giggle.

On the subject of blood tests, I have to say my girlie always had the best HbA1c results in clinic every time. An HbA1c test measures the amount of blood sugar attached to haemoglobin, the part of your red blood cells that carries oxygen from your lungs to the rest of your body, and if it's too high it can cause problems with your feet and sight. Shelbie had her HbA1c checked every three months because of her diabetes, and Dr Bragonier, her endocrinologist, was always a bit surprised by how well her results were. He maintained that her results were always spot on, and better than the other children in clinic who only had diabetes to contend with. Well, that would make perfect sense, wouldn't it? You would expect any child with additional underlying problems to have worse results but, because we are talking about Shelbie, if that's what you were expecting then she would do the opposite.

In September 2011, I went into Shelbie's room to get her up and ready for school. She looked flustered and had a bit of a temperature but would probably have been OK. As it was, I thought that as it was Friday, she could have the day off and then if she was a bit run down, she would have the weekend to recuperate before going back to school on the Monday. Her observations weren't the best throughout the day but there was nothing I was overly concerned about and, come Saturday, she was her usual perky self. Although she still had a bit of a temperature and needed more sleep, she would certainly be OK for school on Monday, I thought, still, perhaps, a little naively.

On Sunday morning I got up to Shelbie at half past four as her monitors were alarming. Her sats were in the seventies. Your sats (saturation level: the oxygen in your blood) are meant to sit at 100%. Shelbie's at that time (because in later years her acceptance sats were a lot lower) were acceptable in the mid-nineties. So, I turned her O_2 up and took her downstairs so the alarms wouldn't wake everyone else. I did her obs and didn't much like the look of her; she seemed really poorly compared to the previous day. Her heart rate was 180, her temperature was over 38°, she was hypothermic and, when I listened to her chest, I could hear crackles on her left lung so assumed she must have a chest infection brewing. As routine I decided to check her BM as well for her blood sugars; she runs in the low teens normally, but now they were twenty-seven. As they were so high, I decided to check her ketone level for ketoacidosis, and this was also worryingly high. I observed her for the next three hours. Knowing Shelbie as I did, I was aware that things could go one way or the other — either get a lot worse, or clear within hours and come to absolutely nothing. But when she was breathing, she was really "blowing out" her breath, as if she was actually out of breath. Her respiratory rate, normally twenty, was now sixty. I emailed Huw Thomas as he knows as well as I that this could come to nothing, and he normally told me to play it out to see how things go. This wasn't a trick she'd tried before, so I was giving her a chance to pull it back. Not that long after emailing him, though, my gut said to take her in regardless, so off we went to ED.

The doctors checked her over and weren't in agreement about the crackles and so said she could return home. Not only did I know she was poorly, but I felt she was deteriorating as the hours passed. I informed them I wasn't taking her home only to be back the next day, so sat in ED for another six hours. Shelbie had typically perked up, which didn't help our cause, and it wasn't unusual for her to think she was funny, but I still knew something wasn't right. I think Shelbie only knew about fighting through things, even when there was an infection or something she kept smiling and fighting through the pain because that's literally all she knew. This, of course, never helped us convince the professionals that there was a problem, but I guess that was how she survived so long. After a while the doctor came back in and said they were admitting her and, after an even longer while, her bed in the ward was finally ready. We took her up there, got her settled, handed over and then headed home. When we left, she seemed stable. We were shattered.

We put the little ones to bed and were just sitting down to watch some TV to de-stress before heading to bed ourselves when the phone rang. It was the ward, telling us we needed to get back to the hospital immediately as Shelbie had deteriorated. When we got back there, she looked grey. She was on fifteen litres of O_2, and despite this her sats weren't staying up. The ward staff contacted outreach to come and assess her (outreach is based in PICU and visit children on wards when there is a concern) and they suggested getting a physiotherapist down to do chest physio and see if it would clear some of those secretions. We sat and waited for the physio, hardly knowing at the time that this was going to be another ride on the train of big battles.

She arrived a little while later. She listened to Shelbie's chest and asked for my initial feelings. I explained that when I'd listened to her chest that morning I could hear crackles on the left lung, but I could be wrong because the ED doctor said there weren't any. She confirmed that this was exactly what she could hear — crackles on the left side — and I was completely correct. 'See,' she said, 'Mum does know best.'

She started some chest physio on Shelbs but there was no improvement so a PICU doctor was called. She decided that Shelbs definitely needed some additional support with her breathing as the O_2 wasn't working, despite her receiving fifteen litres, and explained that they had a new piece of equipment called vapotherm. It was like CPAP — continuous positive airway pressure — but could be delivered via nasal prongs and could be given on the ward as long as Shelbie required no more than eight litres. She went off to see if she could get a machine and also discuss things with other PICU staff because she didn't know Shelbie. She came back shortly afterwards, presumably having spoken to those who do know her, and I instinctively knew what she was about to say. 'I'm really sorry, but we've decided she'll be better off in intensive care.'

It all happened so fast, really. We were told to take her home just that afternoon, and by two a.m. she was in intensive care. My gut feeling not to take her home had been more than justified.

Once we got Shelbie into a bed, she did her usual trick of appearing OK. Her sats were one hundred per cent and she appeared OK. The nurse who had her looked at the doctor a bit baffled. The poor doctor went red and said, 'I know, I know. She's looking fine, but she wasn't like that on the ward.' I chuckled but felt I had to speak up as we weren't fooled by her little tricks any more.

'Don't be fooled. You'll turn your back again and she'll not be breathing at all. You can't trust her!' We stayed with Shelbs a little longer then went to sort the other children out. I went back in first thing and stayed at the hospital while Nick was going back and forth between the hospital and other children.

We had been put on a waiting list to stay at Ronald McDonald house. This was a place just minutes' walk away where you can stay free of charge for as long as your child is ill. They welcomed us all as a family. I stayed at the hospital the first week and then Nick and the children joined me once we had a room there. I'd never appreciated before just how much this house did for you. I had heard of it and knew there was a collection pot if you went to a McDonald's, but didn't know anything about it. The hospital staff had mentioned it to us, and it was a lifesaver. We only had to wait about five days to get our room, Nick went to pick the keys up, and this became our home for now.

The month in PICU was another roller coaster. At two fifteen a.m., just after Shelbie had been admitted to PICU, we contacted the family to say she was in intensive care. The doctors decided it wasn't ketoacidosis, despite her originally high ketone levels, because they had started coming down on their own. They questioned whether the problem was actually to do with her kidneys, because of the kidney problems she had and because her body was swelling, and she was bleeding from her gastrostomy. So we all just waited and kept a close eye on things. We didn't know at the time, but Huw Thomas had brought his thinking cap into work as he often needed to do with Her Ladyship and was already wondering if the acidosis was in fact because of a metabolic disorder. I do briefly remember this being mentioned at some point but everything was a bit of a blur. After a while Shelbie tested positive for flu, but they weren't convinced this was the cause for her visit.

A few days in, her breathing got worse during the night so she was put on BiPAP — Bilevel Positive Airway Pressure — which is a non-invasive ventilation (so she wasn't intubated with a tube into her lungs, but the machine was still doing the breathing for her via a full-face mask). Twenty-four hours later, with no improvement (in fact, only deterioration) they decided to fully ventilate. I just couldn't believe that only days before my little girl was, so-say, just "a bit under the weather.

By three a.m. the following morning, as Shelbie had continued to get worse, they turned the ventilation up to the maximum. The next step was an oscillator. We'd been shown one before but didn't really understand it. We just knew this was the last option, and that if this didn't work, there was no more they could do to keep our princess alive. The following day showed no improvement. They would give her twenty-four hours more, then they wanted to let her go.

Through lots of prayer, Shelbie had a stable night with her O_2 down to fifty per cent and there was talk of tweaking her pressures down. (The percentage was the amount of O_2 being delivered; it's measured differently to when you're on standard O_2 and the pressures are, putting it an easy way, the pressure that is put into the lung to keep it open. But if the pressure is too high the lung can become stiff and then can't deflate.)

I hit a brick wall of being emotionally tired and couldn't cope with any more talk of letting her go. I said to the doctors, 'If you haven't got anything positive to say you're banned from her room.' It was just my way of coping and there are times you can only take hearing so much, especially when it just seemed to be constant problems. Funnily enough, we were left in peace that day.

It didn't last though, Shelbs being stable. She started getting more and more poorly and so was then put on the oscillator. This was by far the worst she had ever been, and we still did not really know what we were dealing with. The oscillator was now explained to us. Where a ventilator opens and closes the lungs as is normal when breathing, an oscillator keeps the lungs open and "shakes" the breath in. I think that's the easiest way to understand it, I'm trying to explain things without it sounding like a medical journal, but the truth is that Shelbie was a medical child, a medical mystery if you will, with very complex medical needs. It wasn't all of who she was, but it was a massive part of her, and as such a massive part of our day-to-day life.

Shelbie's lungs were stiff and, as lungs are delicate like tissue paper, had started tearing. The longer you're ventilated the harder it is for them to recover.

I just felt sick coming in each day and getting more and more bad news. The staff were amazing and a lot knew Shelbie from over the years. But her reputation goes before her, so even staff that hadn't met her had often heard of her. The physios in PICU were second to none. We had had the same one over the years — Christina, and on a few occasions Sophie — and we built quite a good rapport with them as they were visiting Shelbie sometimes three or more times a day and were an integral part of her recovery. These professionals should never be forgotten. Physios don't just hand out exercises for someone with a bad leg. Without these guys the doctors would never get as far as they do with patients. They are just as much lifesavers and we will always be grateful for the care and commitment they gave Shelbs. Chest physio is physically tiring and difficult to perform. It takes a lot of stamina; I used to ache after doing it for Shelbie.

But even with all these people around trying to help her I still felt so alone at times.

While Shelbie was in hospital, we had a lot of people visit, but Pete and Karen, a couple from the other church I had gone to with my brother, were coming in pretty much daily. They were an absolute tower of strength and sometimes I don't think people realise the impact they can have just by being there.

A few days after Shelbie had been put on the oscillator, a prophet rang the pastor of my brother's church and said we had to read two verses from The Bible two to three times a day, as you would take antibiotics, and that this would heal Shelbie if we read it in faith. So, we did this faithfully with help from our dear friend, Margarita, who would read and sit with Shelbie when we were with the other children, taking so much pressure off us. For that I'll always be grateful. I love her for her love for our family. We had prayer going on in lots of different churches, including Australia. I just felt so humbled with the amount of people praying for Shelbs and I do believe strongly in the power of prayer.

There was a time we couldn't turn Shelbie because she was so weak it would make her bradycardic, so the nurse would try to stretch it out to six hours before turning her. Otherwise, it just wasn't worth the risk on her heart. (Her heart was always fine when she was well but became one of the biggest concerns as soon as she became ill.) We were having terrible trouble keeping her blood pressure up, but every time Nick kissed her or if Margarita sang or chatted to her, it would rise. It's surprising how powerful someone's presence can be. I don't think we can ever underestimate the effects we have on people when they are poorly. I think often our love can pull them through just as importantly as any drug they're being given. Even at Shelbie's lowest she was responding to the people she loved.

We continued reading the verses. Luke 11:1–13:

One day Jesus was praying in a certain place. When He finished, one of His disciples said to Him, 'Lord, teach us to pray, just as John taught his disciples.'

He said to them, 'When you pray, say: father, hallowed be your name, your kingdom come. Give us each day our daily bread. Forgive us our sins, for we also forgive everyone who sins against us. And lead us not into temptation.'

Then Jesus said to them, 'Suppose you had a friend, and you go to him at midnight and say "friend, lend me three loaves of bread; a friend of mine on a journey has come to me, and I have no food to offer him."

'And suppose the one inside answers, "Don't bother me. The door is already locked, and my children and I are in bed. I can't get up and give you anything." I tell you, even though he won't get up and give you the bread because of friendship, yet because of your shameless audacity he will surely get up and give you as much as you need.

'So I say to you: ask and it will be given to you; seek and you will find; knock and the door will be opened to you. For everyone who asks receives; the one who seeks finds; and to the one who knocks, the door will be opened.

'Which of you fathers, if your son asks for a fish, will give him a snake instead? Or if he asks for an egg, will give him a scorpion? If you then, though you are evil, know how to give good gifts to your children, how much more will your Father in Heaven give the Holy Spirit to those who ask him?'

And also Isaiah 53:1–12:

Who hath believed our report? And to whom is the arm of the LORD revealed? For he shall grow up before him as a tender plant, and as a root out of a dry ground: he hath no form nor comeliness; and when we shall see him, there is no beauty that we should desire him. He is despised and rejected of men; a man of sorrows, and acquainted with grief: and we hid as it were our faces from him; he was despised, and we esteemed him not. Surely he hath borne our griefs, and carried our sorrows: yet we did esteem him stricken, smitten of god, and afflicted. But he was wounded form our transgressions, he was bruised for our iniquities: chastisement of our peace was upon him; and with his stripes we are healed. All we like sheep have gone astray; we have turned everyone to his own way; and the Lord hath laid on him the iniquity of us all. He was oppressed and he was afflicted, yet he opened not his mouth: he is brought as a lamb to the slaughter, and as sheep before her shearers is dumb, so he openeth not his mouth. He was taken from prison and from judgement: and who shall declare his generation? For he was cut off out of the land of the living: for the transgression of my people was he stricken. And he made his grave with the wicked, and with the rich in his death; because he had done no violence, neither was any deceit in his mouth. Yet it pleased the Lord to bruise him; he hath put him to grief: when thou shalt make his soul an offering for sin, he shall see his seed, he shall prolong his days, and the pleasure of the Lord shall prosper in his hand. He shall see of the travail of his soul, and shall be satisfied: by his knowledge shall my righteous servant justify many; for he shall bear their iniquities. Therefore will I divide him a portion with the great, and he shall divide the spoil with the strong; because he hath poured out his soul unto death: and he was numbered with the transgressors; and he bears the sin of many, and made intercession for the transgressors.

These two readings didn't speak to me at all. I seemed to have a mental block as I wasn't really understanding what they were saying, and especially how they were connected to Shelbie in any way. I guess that's the beauty of my faith. I don't have to understand or get it all, I just have to trust and believe, so I continued reading them regardless. I guessed at some stage it would make sense when I needed to understand it. One verse I did read often which I found comforted me was Psalm 116:1–9:

I love the Lord, because he has heard my voice and supplications.

Because He has inclined His ear unto me, therefore will I call upon Him as long as I live.

The sorrows of death compassed me, and the pains of hell got hold upon me: I found trouble and sorrow.

Then I called upon the name of the Lord, I beseech, deliver my soul.

Gracious is the Lord, and righteous; our god is merciful.

The Lord preserveth the simple: I was brought low, and He helped me.

Return unto thy rest, o my soul; for the Lord hath dealt bountifully with thee.

For thou hast delivered my soul from death, mine eyes from tears, and my feet from falling.

I will walk before the Lord in the land of the living.

About a week after being on the oscillator, Shelbs' left lung had completely collapsed. Talking to Pete and Karen they asked if I had a feeling what was going to happen and I said, 'I honestly think this is it: she will never come home.' She's a fighter through and through but how can anyone pull through with so much wrong, and with the doctors still not knowing exactly what they were treating?

Dr Grant came in one morning and admitted that they didn't know what else they could do or what they were carrying on for. 'I started Shelbie on steroids yesterday and I will give her a week tops, but realistically I expect an improvement in forty-eight hours. If by next

Monday we don't feel we're getting anywhere we've come to the end.' Just days before we had this chat, I had been reading the verses from The Bible with my hand on Shelbs' chest, as usual, when it felt like there was a hand on top of mine. I felt it was God's hand, as I was praying for healing. It reminded me to have faith and for the first time I felt maybe she would beat this. But then that night her O_2 had to be put up, and afterwards we'd had this dreaded discussion. I didn't know if it was a test of faith or Satan getting desperate.

Pete remarked that, 'Feeling a hand on top of yours could be God saying, "I'm with you, I'm here. Shelbie's life for you is faith and your life a life of faith for her. Satan can sling his hook. You're God's daughter through and through and He loves you so much".' That helped me carry on. Pete kept reminding me not to do it by my own strength but by God's and as I looked at my little girl, I knew the only definite was God being there, holding us, loving us.

For two days running after that chat with the doctor, Shelbie's chest X-rays (which she was having daily) were looking better. Her blood gases — indications of infections — were holding fast, certainly not getting any worse. They started tweaking her O_2 and pressures down and her delta p (that's the amount they are keeping her lungs open). This was such a huge turn around in such a short time.

Two days after that dreaded talk, Shelbie went back onto the ventilator, the following day she was pushing against my hand with her foot and starting to open her eyes — we were buzzing! When ventilated, Shelbs was given morphine to keep her comfortable, midazolam to keep her sedated and vek to paralyse her: patients have short periods of being taken off the vek to make sure they are still moving their limbs, etc., which is distressing to watch, but necessary. Shelbie would always have tears rolling down her cheeks when they did it. But this was the most she had responded when having her break from the drug.

Our physio, Christina, knowing Shelbie so well, knew when and how far to push Madam and decided that if she stayed this stable, they would extubate the following day: it was scheduled for eleven a.m., for her then to go onto BiPAP again.

The following day Shelbie showed off and went straight onto vapotherm. She struggled overnight so went on CPAP but that was just a tiny setback because just three days after going back onto ventilation from the oscillator, she had been extubated. I mean, this was massive! When she decided she was going to turn it around, man, she did just that!

A few days after she went back to the ward, being supported by PICU staff, and slowly started sucking her thumb once more and yawning. This should be so natural, shouldn't it, but she would lose these simple abilities through illness and we could never assume she would regain them, so whatever she did manage was an achievement. The withdrawal symptoms from the strong drugs she had been on was heart-breaking to watch and lasted many weeks but, that aside, our precious girl was still alive and, for now, out of danger. She eventually went back onto vapotherm and when she came home a month later, she was just on the O_2.

It was fantastic to get her home but so, so tiring. She was still to be closely monitored which Nick and I were taking in turns to do at night. Everyone just assumes people are fine when they're sent home, but that's not the case. There was a long way to go and her care was still quite intense. In fact, that's probably the one time you need the support the most, more than when they're actually in hospital. I remember walking around like a zombie. Everyone you bumped into, or people who messaged, would be buzzing for you. 'Oh, she's home, that's great.' And it was. But we were still coming to terms with her being alive. It's a bit crazy because Shelbs had got over whatever illness she'd had and was bouncing around but we were always a good few steps behind her, trying to process what we had just been through, still working out whether it was OK to breathe now, and not quite believing she was still alive given what she had just gone through and how close she was to death.

Looking At You

(written one time Shelbie was in hospital and I was trying to express to her how she made me feel)

When I look into your eyes
I see something more precious than gold
You were sent here for a reason
For me to have and to hold

I sit with you on my lap
You don't understand the pain
You think it's supposed to be that way
It's not, that wasn't the aim

When you're peacefully sleeping
I sit there a while watching you
You smile, you play, you clap your hands
It can't last but you haven't a clue

When you're not here I can smell you
I can't hold you but I can see your face
The way you move, how you enjoy life
Doing everything at your own steady pace

I could burst with love for you
I will protect you 'til the day I die
I can't stop what's going to happen
When it's right, I'll explain — I won't lie

There's one promise that I can make
To love you and always be here
And when it's time for you to go
This will be done without any fear.

Chapter Seven

The first time I went to Ronald McDonald House, Nick had to get back to be with the other children so I took the few clothes I had with me up to my room and then went down to the kitchen for a cuppa and a cigarette. This was the first time I had been away from Shelbie and I needed to have a little while to just breathe!

I noticed a lot of people outside in the back garden as I waited for the kettle to boil and must admit that I was a bit nervous. It can be daunting going into a house with a load of strangers at a time when you are feeling so vulnerable yourself. It was also a bit alien — you're there with so many different people (there are twenty bedrooms, so this place is serving twenty families) who all have different stories, different experiences, and different roads they've travelled yet, somehow, they were all in a similar position to me.

As I went out with my coffee a man stood up and introduced himself and everyone else there too, instantly putting me at ease. His name was Tim, his partner was Gina, and although sadly these guys aren't together any more, we are still in contact with them years later. I recognised some of the parents by sight from PICU, other families had babies in NICU (the neonatal version). Everyone was so friendly and so supportive. On the days when things were difficult there was always someone to listen, and other times, when you were having a more stable day, you would be the one doing the listening. We needed to laugh and still feel human at times, and I think that's often the only way to get through — even if it's only for a few hours. There was in fact a lot of laughter (even when it didn't always seem appropriate) and there were also tears, as our little ones would pick up, then take a dip, then pick up again…

Our niece, Teigan, who was just coming up to seven, had been admitted to hospital just before Shelbs left PICU, so my brother and sister-in-law, Matt and Laura, also spent a lot of time at the house. Teigan had severe Crohn's disease. We would help each other out with babysitting as Matt and Laura had a three-year-old, Cowen, as well. I think all the cousins being together gave them all a bit of support.

The day after we'd got the keys to Ronald McDonald House, Nick and I went to pick the children up from school and packed some clothes and toys and brought them back as this was going to be home for now. Rhys was an adult by this point and Connor didn't want to stay at the hospital, so friends had Connor while Rhys stayed at home with some other friends just looking out for him. Eventually Courtney stayed with friends too so she could continue school, but she spent a few weeks with us. It was manic having one double bed and one single mattress for six of us, but it didn't matter — we managed, as we all just wanted to be together. And a few weeks after arriving, we were given a bigger room, anyway.

Kal and Mac went to hospital school and Cienna, too young for school, went to the play centre in hospital each day which gave us time with Shelbie on our own. We would take her brothers and sister in for just a short while each time. They could see for themselves how she was and ask any questions they had but we couldn't expect them to just sit there quietly. They were young children, and we still had to consider them as well.

Eventually more families were bringing their other children in. I remember one family saying their children weren't coping being away from Mummy and Daddy, so I suggested they brought them to stay. This couple were a bit sceptical as they didn't want to impose on the house or have their kids miss school. I just reminded them that, firstly, the staff would welcome them because they would understand how important it was to all be together whenever possible and, secondly, there was a hospital school and education comes nowhere close compared to a family needing each other: there was always time to catch up if needs be. Then the trend seemed to follow around the house and more and more families were bringing the siblings in, which to be honest is often the thing a poorly child needs. Even if they're unconscious or have limited understanding, having the people they know, love and trust with them is the best medicine. It was fantastic to see this house filling up with little people, putting smiles on the adults' faces. The children all built friendships and more and more children were going off together to school or the play centre.

Tim and Gina become close friends and we would take it in turns to babysit if the children were too tired to go to evening Radio Lollipop, another session where you could leave your children for a few hours and be with your poorly one. It's surprising how you build a friendship with someone so quickly when you spend day-in-day-out with them. We probably spent more hours with everyone in the house, especially Gina and Tim, than we did with friends we had known for years. In just days people would recognise your vulnerabilities, your strengths and your weaknesses, and they would laugh with you and cry with you. You wouldn't have the energy to not open up completely if you'd had a bad day so other people saw every colour of you in a short space of time. It often takes months, if not years, to get to that place with a friend in ordinary circumstances, but here you didn't have the strength or time to hold back so you formed those bonds very quickly. When we eventually went home with Shelbs, we would still go back to the house to see everyone until Gina and Tim left.

It was fantastic going home — of course it was — but it was so lonely too. We didn't have the medical support any more and we also missed the emotional support, and that carries you miles, believe me. It was such a weird feeling. For over six weeks there had always been someone around — even if the other families weren't about, the staff were — so being in an empty house, the children all back in their school routines, was unnerving. Everyone just helped each other survive. There were some people that wanted to just keep to themselves and that's fine too, we all deal with these trying times differently, but on the whole, we were like a little family for a short while, which is paramount, especially for those whose other family didn't manage to get to visit.

Back home once more, I found my emotions were on a constant roller coaster, trying to deal with what had been happening over those past weeks and months. The stable moments, when you are either waiting for the next illness or you dare to maybe just get a little comfortable, and then your child can throw a wobbly and you're back on that roller coaster ride, going very fast and seemingly out of control. It can drive you a little mad sometimes so I guess the only way to deal with it is to revel in the good times, grabbing them tight with both hands. Maybe we should all live by Shelbie's motto: *Every day is a blast. Live for the moment, as we don't know how many "moments" we have. So let's just have fun, fun, fun!*

While we were at Ronald McDonald House, Cienna had her third birthday and family and friends came for a little tea party. She had a lovely day and a cake in the play centre. She asked me about eight months later, 'Am I having my birthday at home or in hospital this time?' Bless. She was planning ahead! I told her she would have to ask Shelbs for the answer on that one, and she just chuckled.

Mac banged his face while playing on the bed and ended up in ED, and has a beautiful little scar on his cheek as a reminder. Teigan, still an inpatient, had a little seventh birthday tea with us at the house as well, coming out of hospital for just a few hours to join us. Whatever is going on in everyday life still has to continue to a degree, when possible, and you can still make things happen by working around it. It's just done in a different way to everyone else. We improvise and compromise!

One particular text I had when Shelbie was in was from my uncle Neil, my dad's brother. It read:

Our thoughts are with you all. You have strength of character that far exceeds your age. Your father would be proud of you.

They were just a few simple words, but they carried me not just in hospital but also for months after we got home. Not because I think I am anything special — I'm not, I'm just a mum doing her job — but because someone saw something that made him feel those words were fitting, and that meant that someone believed in me. It gives you that extra boost you need to keep going, to keep fighting. When all your energy seems to have gone, someone expressing their faith in you is enough to push you that little bit further.

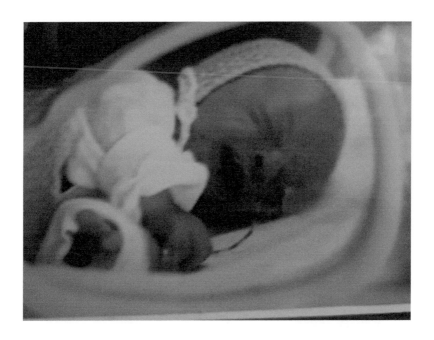

Above: February 1995. This is Charlie. He wasn't fed for the first few days so he was hungry and grizzly.

Below: February 1995. But settled with a little side rub.

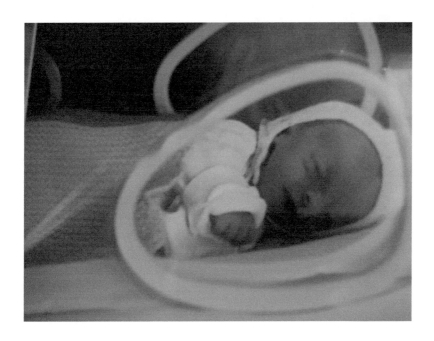

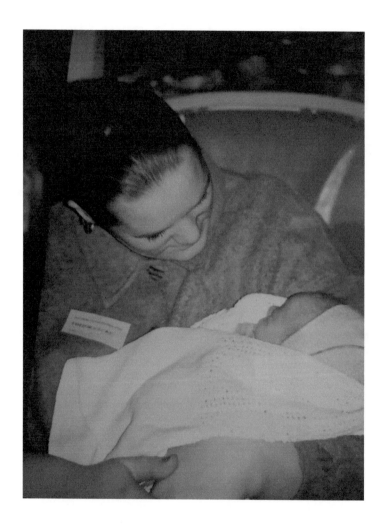

February 1995. The first time I held him at a few weeks old

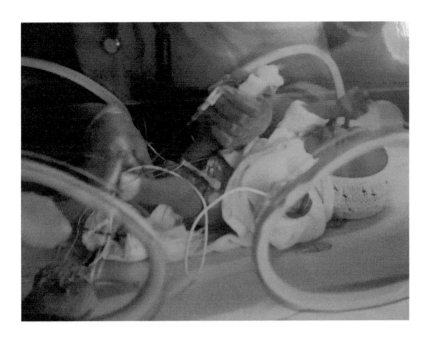

Above: February 1995. Charlie a few weeks old in SCBU

Below: March 1995. Charlie a few weeks after he came out of
SCBU

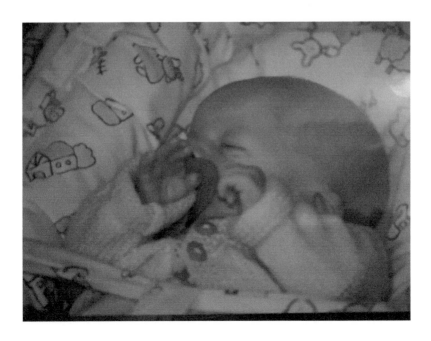

Above: March 1995. Rhys giving out his brotherly love.

Below: April 1995. The only time Charlie looked happy and
contented was in the water like his little sister.

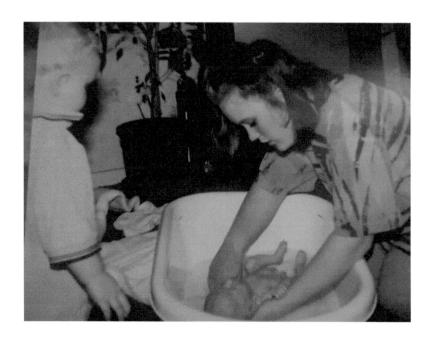

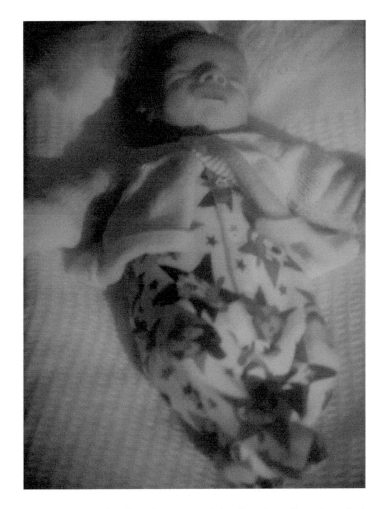

March 1995. Enjoying the sun and the freedom from hospital.

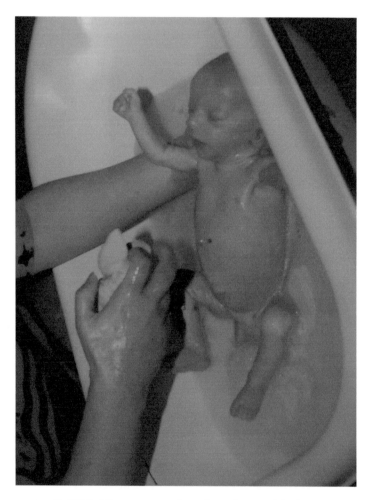

April 1995. You can see the relaxation on his face

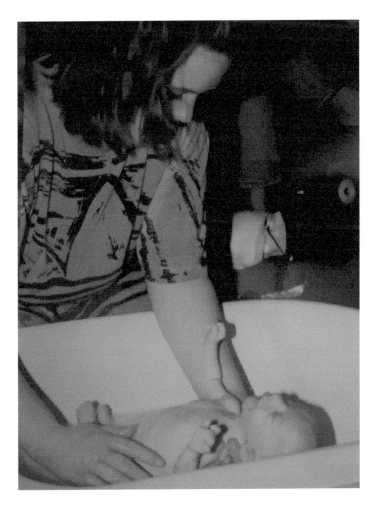

Bath time. April 1995

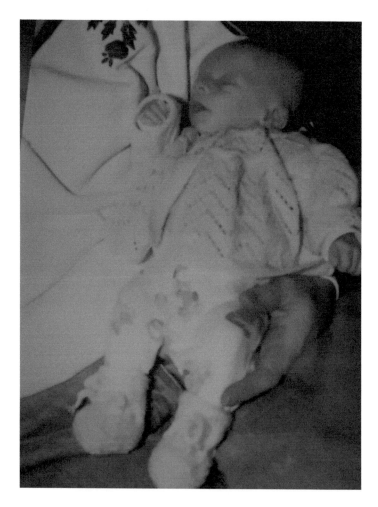

April 1995. And all settled after his bath.

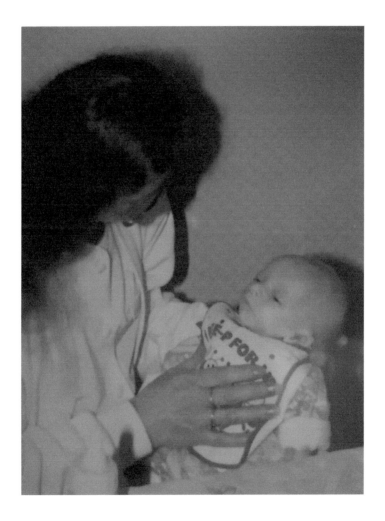

April 1995. My mum holding Charlie at Easter time. The only
time he had his eyes open before his op.

December 1999. Shelbie at a few weeks old

Summer 2000. Rhys, Connor, Courtney and Shelbie

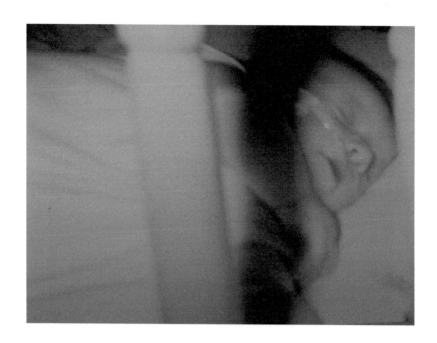

Above: Summer 2000. Shelbs

Below: November 2000. Shelbie a week before her first
birthday in PICU with a partial lung collapse

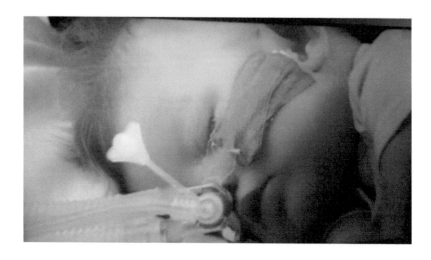

2000 Me and Shelbs

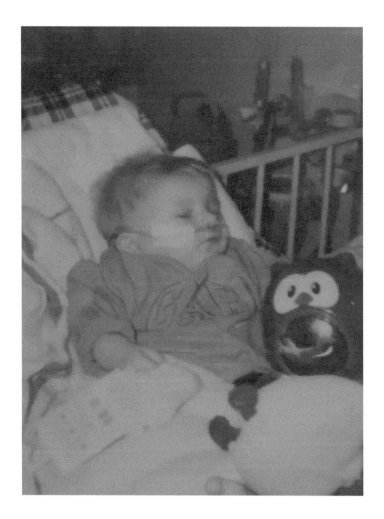

November 2000. Shelbie's first birthday out of PICU and back
on the baby ward.

July 2001. Shelbie's dedication

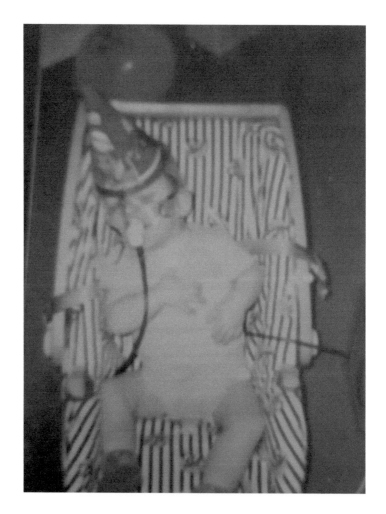

November 2001 Shelbie's second birthday in hospital.

Above: June 2002. Paignton Zoo

Below: 2002. Courtney and Shelbie with Grampy (my dad)

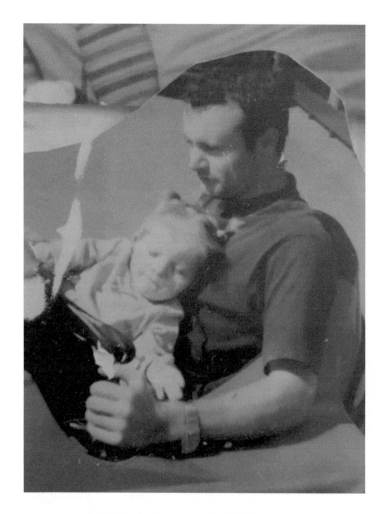

2002. A day out with Daddy

Above: November 2002. Me and Nick with Rhys, Shelbie,
Courtney and Connor

Below: November 2002

2004 Shelbie and Rhys

July 2004 On holiday in Cornwall (Courtney and Shelbie)

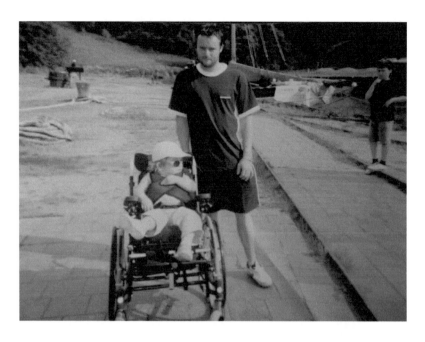

Above: July 2004 On holiday in Cornwall with Daddy

Below: November 2004. Connor and Shelbs playing with her
new birthday toys

Above: 2005 A day out with school. Playing in the water with Margarita

Below: Summer 2005 On holiday in Kidwelly with Aunty Emma

Above: Summer 2005 Shelbs on holiday in Kidwelly with Rhys
and Courtney

Below: 2006 On holiday at butlins

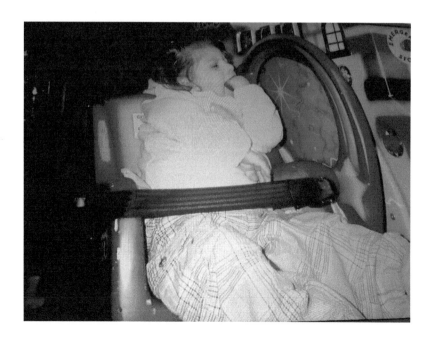

2005 Shelbie and Courtney

Above: 2006 Having fun in school

Below: June 2006 After watching the FA Cup with Daddy

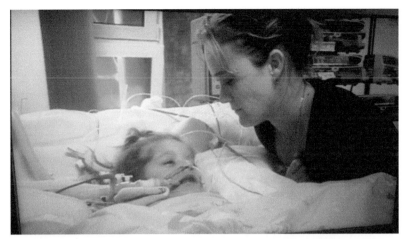

January 2008. Shelbie in PICU (paediatric intensive care unit) after her bowel operation

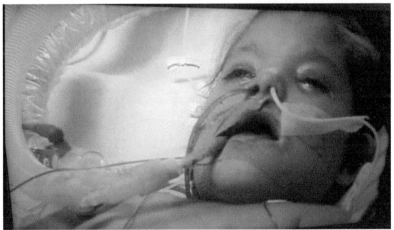

The hardest times to see her were when she cried, but couldn't communicate. She never gave up in a fight

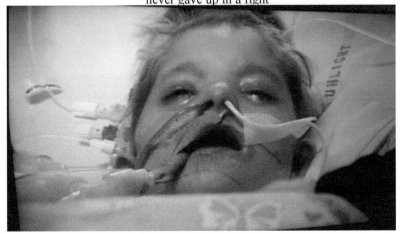

November 2008 Shelbie, Kalan, Mackenzie and Cienna

August 2009 Shelbie with Kalan, sitting in her armchair with her, which was a regular occurrence

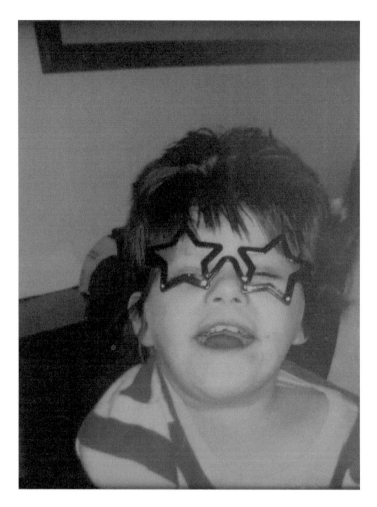

2011. At a cousin's birthday party

June 2011 School sports day with Margarita

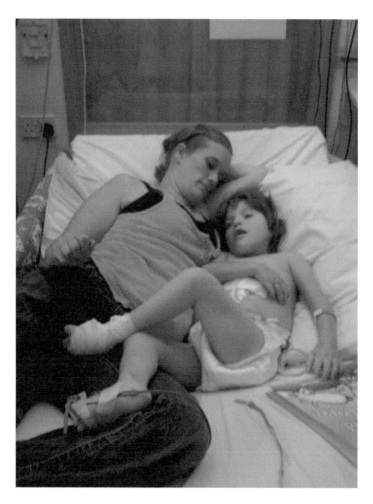

August 2010 Shelbs still in hospital having a 'cwtch' with
mummy

August 2011 At the local park with Mum and Cienna

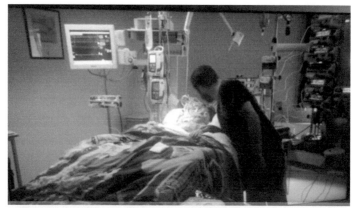

September 2011 You get some idea of how many syringe drivers were delivering drugs to keep her alive. At one point there was twelve going at once, not including her regular drugs she was on anyway

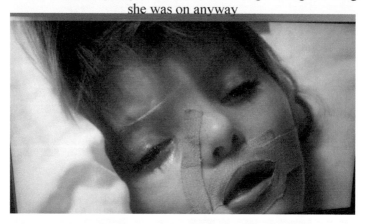

September 2011 One of our toughest PICU admissions. This admission was never quite clear as to why her breathing was so bad. But it resulted on her being in an oscillator

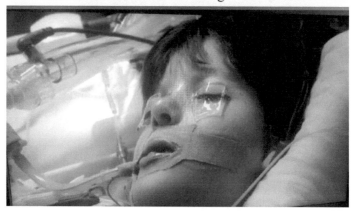

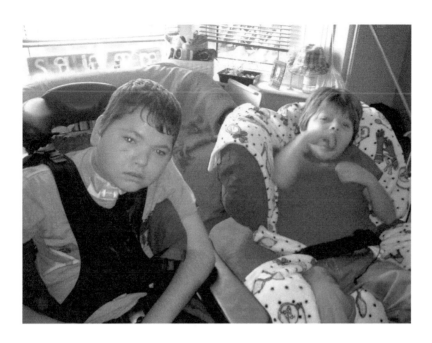

Above: July 2012 Shelbs and Mitchell

Below: November 2012. Shelbie's 13th birthday.

Above: 2013 Getting ready for surfing with Cienna, courtesy of
Nick Thorn surfing school in Devon

Below: 2013. Surfing with Daddy

Above: 2014. A walk in the forest of Dean

Below: May 2014. Shelbie's baptism.

2015 Having fun swimming at school

October 2015. Sunday afternoon snuggles with Mum and
Sophia

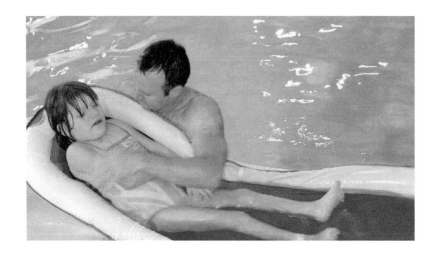

Above: November 2015. Whitemead for 16th birthday.

Below: November 2015. Shelbs 16th birthday with Aunty Emma.

December 2015 Christmas at Whitemead. My favourite part of
the day, rolling around in all the wrapping paper

December 2015. Cuddles with Kalan after her beer.

Above: December 2015. Santa visit through Ty Hafan hospice

Below: January 2016 Sarah the play worker at Bristol children's hospital letting Shelbs enjoy the sensory lights in her room on an admission

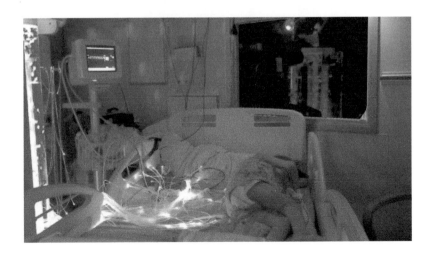

January 2016 Mac and Cienna entertaining themselves in Shelbs
hospital room

March 2016 Shelbs with Cienna on our way to a stay at LBH
(Little Bridge House)

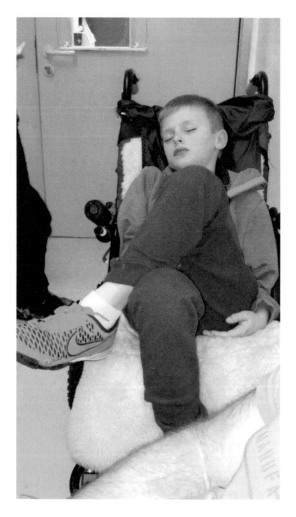

March 2016 Kalan waiting in Emergency department for Shelbs to be admitted.

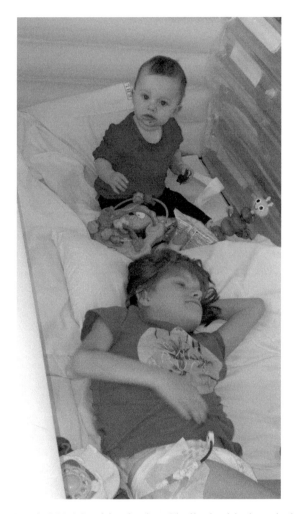

March 2016 Sophia sharing Shelbs bed in hospital

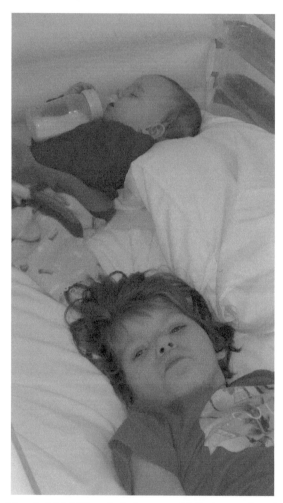

March 2016 Hospital days could feel very long!

June 2017 Ready for a walk with dad

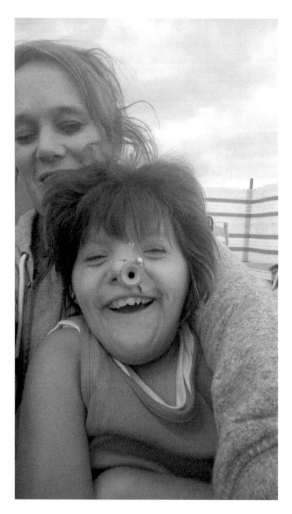

September 2017 At the beach, on holiday in Devon

Above: March 2018 Shelbs on an Easter egg hunt at LBH with
Kalan, Mac, Cienna, Sophia and William and Lewis and their
siblings Chloe and Oliver

Below: June 2018. Shelbs neices, Sophia and Aria and sister
Cienna at LBH.

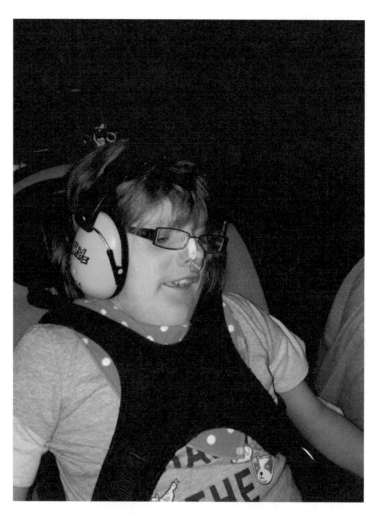

July 2018. Hillsong conference

July 2018. A day trip out while at Whitemead to Perry Grove
railway with our friends Justin, Leah and Mike.

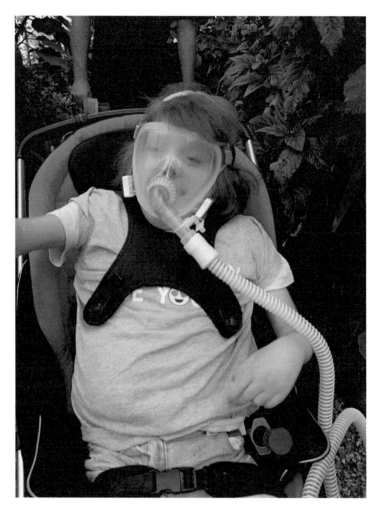

August 2018 Still enjoying the butterfly zoo

August 2018 Chilling after coming out of the butterfly zoo

August 2018 Having fun with Kalan and Cienna

September 2018. Aria pushing Shelbs on the swing at Whitemead

September 2018 Shelbs waiting to go to school in her post 16
uniform

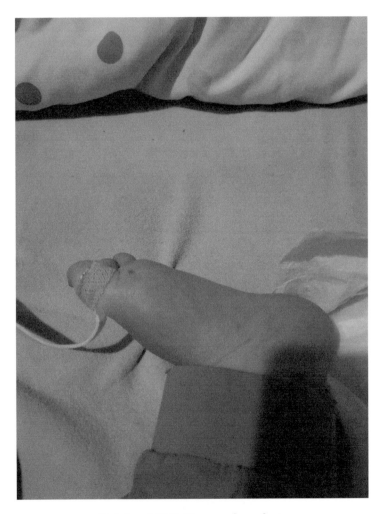

October 2018. Her precious feet.

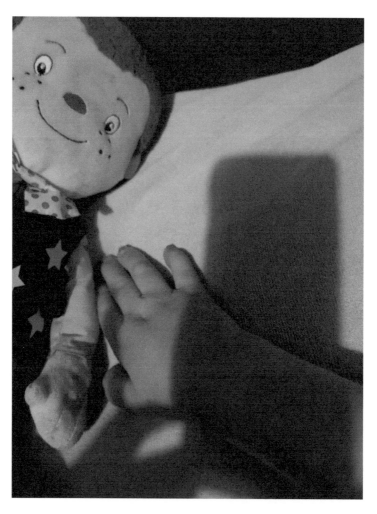

October 2018. Her scrummy chubby hand

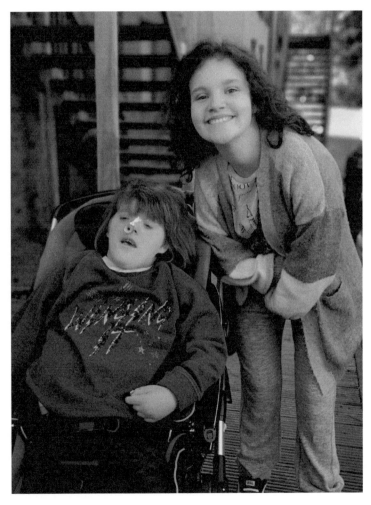

October 2018. Before we left Whitemead Shelbs and Zoe had their picture taken.. Shelbs wasn't well on this weekend away. Her little body was up and down, getting more and more tired

November 2018. Whitemead swim

November 2018. Time for a cuppa in the restaurant

November 2018. Shelbie and Cienna waiting for a ride to start

November 2018. On the slinky ride with Nick and Mac

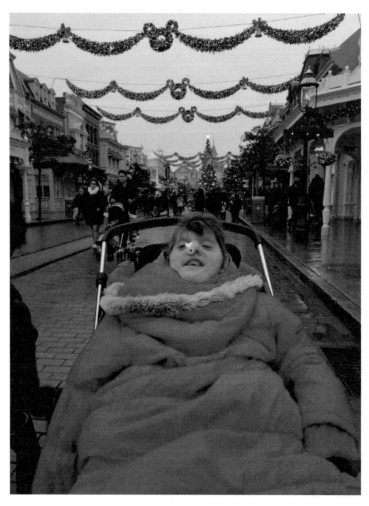

November 2018. Shelbie loved walking through the streets with all the hussle and bussle

November 2018. Sophia and Aria enjoying being in Disneyland
with Shelbie

Above: November 2018. Enjoying the rides, thanks to Magic moments charity. Me, Shelbie and Sophia.

Below: November 2018. Recovering from a very busy holiday

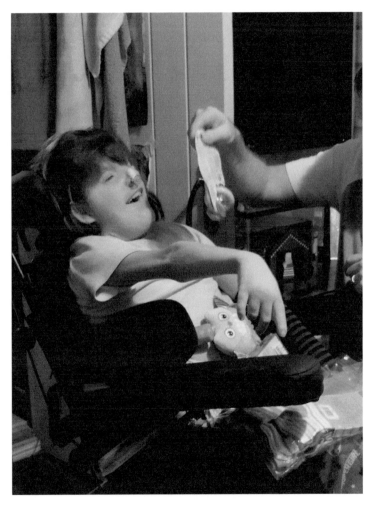

December 2018. Shelbs enjoying all her new toys. We were
pleased she was really well for this day

December 2018. Getting full up and very happy, not knowing at
this time that this would be her last Christmas

December 2018. Shelbs loved her siblings cuddling with her

February 2019. Shelbs with dad and Aria

February 2019. Shelbs and Mac ice skating in Cardiff

March 2019. Me and Shelbs on Mother's day, 2 weeks before
she died. She was getting so tired by this point.

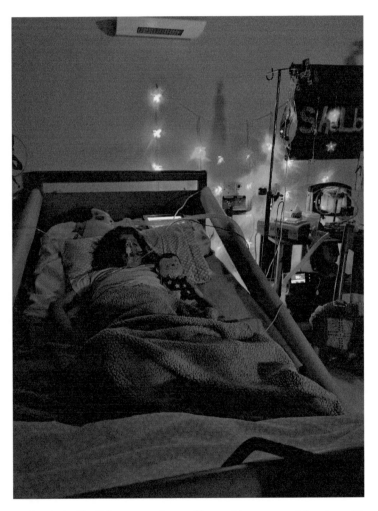

April 2019. Shelbie was only settling with me cwtching her. To
slip away I would have to place Mr Tumble by her.

April 2019. This is the beautiful room 'star born' where Shelbie
rested after she had died. Its important to not be afraid to show
this picture. We've shown our children there is nothing to be
fearful of, as death is natural and not to be feared. They were
comfortable coming in this room

Above: April 2019. This is Shelbie's 'rainbow bed' as Sophia calls it. The children decorated her name themselves, we had these instead of flowers.

Below: April 2019. Shelbie's beautiful Urn to match her rainbow bed, alongside her rainbow roses tied by her NPA tape.

Above: June 2020. Another angle of the sensory room with
some new lights and some of Shelbie's old ones. Plus the ball pit
is made out of her old bed surround.

Below: June 2020. And we have decided to dedicate it 'Shelbie's
space'. This sign is something Courtney made for Shelbie's
bedroom many years before.

May 2021. Nellie was born five weeks after Shelbie died. The grandchildren have been a welcomed distraction to help in our healing. (Aria, Nellie and Sophia.)

Chapter Eight

In January 2012 Shelbie went back to school, just doing four short days so she had the middle of the week to build her energy back up. Slowly we had our little princess back, and it took a long time for her to get her voice back, but she did it. Her sats were never as good as before and she had a lot more fits and cyanosed episodes — when she went blue due to not having enough oxygen of the blood — but for someone who was meant to be dead I didn't think things were all that bad, all things considered!

Shelbs continued loving life. Blowing kisses and raspberries, clapping, singing, saying, 'Mamma Mamma', rolling around — all the things she loved in life were still there. Life plodded along with a few admissions, which wasn't bad for the young lady, but we did notice since she had come out of PICU that she was bruising a lot more, and very easily, too. She used to kick ten bells out of solid units and suchlike and never even marked, so this was out of her norm. Doctors said they would keep a close eye on this.

Shelbs went in for a routine tube change, as her JEJ feeding tube was broken, and Miss McNally was taking her to theatre for this. Halfway through the procedure the nurse came in to Nick and me and said, 'Miss McNally wants to see you in theatre now.' I felt sick, I was shaking. I thought Shelbie must be dying down there. Why else would she call us down halfway through the procedure?

Miss McNally told us that Shelbie was bleeding internally. She wasn't sure if she had nicked something but she was giving her twenty minutes for the bleed to stop; if it didn't, she was going to open her up completely. We knew this was a big risk as her stomach had never been as it should since her bowel surgery, but there was no choice as otherwise she would bleed to death. We waited outside the theatre and after thirty minutes the bleeding stopped. They'd realised her platelets were too low.

She had been having low platelets, but no one had checked them before surgery so Nick and I made sure in the future to double-check this whenever she needed a procedure. It was just one of those things that happens, but if we could stay on the ball, it meant we would have one less scare each time. The operation couldn't go ahead as they had to wait for Shelbie to stabilise; it took place five days later. While we were waiting to go to theatre this second time, Shelbie managed to bite her new cannula in half. It had only just been replaced and was her third line that day. The doctors weren't overly impressed by what I'm sure she thought was her apparent hilarious behaviour.

A few months after this drama, Father's Day was approaching. Shelbie had not been herself she was obviously in pain but the doctors couldn't do anything as they couldn't ascertain what the problem was. So Father's Day wasn't the best it could have been as she was so unhappy and uncomfortable. The following weekend I had Teigan and Cowen staying over, and all the kids wanted to go to church although I wasn't particularly in the right headspace for it. I was tired and irritable and didn't think it was fair to be around anyone. I'm snappy when I'm tired, and we had had sleepless nights with Shelbie's pain and so, emotionally, I wasn't in the best place. Things just catch up with you sometimes and you need to work through it to get to where you need to be, but the children insisted on going so I took them.

The kids all went out to 'kids' church' and pastor John started talking. 'Do you feel you're worthless, do you feel unloved, do you feel you're not a good Christian/person?' It's not God, I realised, who tells you this, it's Satan who makes you feel this way. Your actions can make you feel crap. It felt like John was describing the past week of how I had felt. I just sat there sobbing. A friend asked if I was OK.

I said, 'Do you ever feel like you're drowning?' Then, as I continued talking, I realised I was feeling so low because the realisation had come that we were starting to lose our precious girl. I had told people that there had been an obvious worsening for the past year, not making the connection that her deterioration meant that we were losing her. Not necessarily within those coming months, it may take years, but it was starting.

This was so hard to swallow. I couldn't be angry with God, as we knew the score all along; we were on borrowed time. I could say it, talk about it, but to actually let my mind accept it was a whole new ball game. Now it was starting to sink in, but although I didn't get angry with God, I didn't want to deal with it either. I just couldn't be bothered with anything for days. People I normally pray for didn't get prayer. I was emotionally switched off. Shelbs then ended up back in hospital, she had low sats, high BMs, a temperature, lethargy — pretty much the usual stuff as she had another chest infection.

I prayed she would be all right, but had been a bit "silent" with God. Then something just hit me. I realised that whatever I was or wasn't going through, other people needed prayer regardless. It wasn't easy but it comes back to walking in faith. Yes, I wasn't feeling the best, didn't have control over the situation, didn't like where this was going, but I had to leave it for Him to decide and work on. I didn't have to do anything but trust. So that's what I started to do.

When Shelbie was in with her chest infection, a consultant came to see us and mentioned this metabolic disease again. After tests and in-depth conversations about Shelbie's past history of illnesses, and abilities to do things which she then lost, and just her general day-to-day life from the start, it was decided that Shelbie would have skin and muscle biopsies and a bone marrow test. The results took months to come back, and when they did, they proved inconclusive, but with all the history and other medical factors it was pointing to Shelbie having mitochondrial cytopathy. There's no cure, and it was nothing to do with her Trisomy — just pure bad luck to have another condition — but it was more the mitochondrial making her ill than the Trisomy. There was no medication to stop the progression or to fix her, but they started her on two new drugs anyway. They told us there was little evidence that these drugs did much, but we should give it a go anyway. By this time Shelbie was on forty or more drugs so a few more weren't going to make much difference. She was already rattling like a toy with all the pills inside her, and her bedroom was a mini — or maybe not so mini! — pharmacy. There were also drugs she couldn't be on because of the new diagnosis, like the sodium valproate for her epilepsy, so the medication had to be altered but we managed to get it worked out. Shelbie had been waiting for these tests but Dr Thomas rang and said he wanted them done quickly after a blood result had come back showing that her platelets were far too low. He wanted her straight in for a transfusion. This phone call came just days before Shelbie's thirteenth birthday, although we didn't get the results until months after.

We had decided for Shelbs' thirteenth to throw a massive party. After her big illness we weren't going to rely on waiting for her to have her eighteenth when she was actually eighteen. We agreed that'd we celebrate when she hit her teens which, to be fair, we didn't think she would even be around for. So we were going to celebrate big time! Then, following this phone call we thought, 'Great, she probably isn't even going to make the party.'

We took her in for her transfusion and she was home in time but not particularly happy. She was often grumpy after transfusions. But the party went ahead and it was fantastic. We had an entertainer who did games and music and Shelbie, despite not being one hundred per cent, still managed to have a relatively good time, with Kalan being her bodyguard all night — he didn't leave her side, really. We had noticed since PICU that he'd become a lot more protective of her. He would often sleep in her room and didn't much want to leave her side at home.

So, we now had a new condition to contend with, and I felt like it was another death sentence hanging over her head. I thought she would have to fight double the amount to survive, but Nick saw it differently, simply saying that it didn't change the way we care for her and it didn't change her fight for life. And he was right. She had this condition before it was diagnosed and was fighting anyway, so, actually, in that respect, what was different? As always, as long as Shelbie wanted to fight, we would continue to fight with her.

It can feel very lonely sometimes when you have to digest things and no one can change those results or take that worry away. It's only human to have these feelings, but I guess I was starting to understand that while it was OK, I could actually turn some of that loneliness to someone who could replace it with peace. Being a Christian isn't about knowing all there is to know, it's about learning along the way and changing step by step, day by day. From a human point of view though, no one really understands your heartache except those who have been or are going through a similar story. It's you, the parent, who has to make such life changing, heart-wrenching and sometimes painful decisions and it doesn't make you a crap person by feeling you're not quite in the room sometimes along with everyone else. It's sometimes hard to thank God for everything when you feel that what is so precious to you is slipping away, but blaming Him isn't going to change what's happening. You're just turning away the only one who can keep you going when you're ready to drop.

So Shelbs has managed to bag herself yet another complication? I shouldn't really be surprised, should I!

Each life is a miracle, I have always looked at it like that, and now we were expecting another baby. When we told people, some thought we were mad. Yes, maybe, but not because of having a large family, because I always felt lucky. Some people struggle to be able to have one child, I had been blessed with many. But this little life wasn't to be. We were staying at Little Bridge House, the children's hospice and, at thirteen weeks, I lost the baby and nearly my own life, too. I haemorrhaged and it was the most terrifying time of my life — for myself, anyway. I've obviously been scared for Shelbie countless times. The hospital I went to tried removing the baby while I was still awake and they had given me no painkillers at all, not even Entonox. It was terrifying. I have never in my life felt so much pain. I felt like someone was actually ripping me apart, and had nightmares and sleepless nights for months after. It's strange, isn't it, because if anyone had put Shelbie through that I would have marched them out of her room, but I was in and out of consciousness and feeling very vulnerable. I hope by being at Shelbie's side Nick and I had helped her not have those feelings. I hope that, although sometimes things hurt, she felt safe that we were there and knew we wouldn't allow her to go through any pain unnecessarily. But I thought I was going to die. I know I was close, but I thank God I didn't. Telling the children was heart-breaking, and they were devastated. We had only told them a week or so before, as we were approaching the twelve-week mark.

I was so grateful to be alive to see the children I already have, grow up. But emotionally the loss was so painful, and the emptiness could sometimes feel overbearing. I understand that not all lives are meant to be on earth, but seeing my children suffer kills me. Kalan seemed to be the most affected. He was only seven years old and has a real heart for children and babies — he is so natural with them and so he was the most excited about a new baby. His behaviour had been difficult since PICU and now this was just another thing he had to deal with. I get why he was difficult but he still needed those boundaries, along with a lot of love and reassurance. Once, we were chatting as he had had a particularly bad day and he turned to me and said, 'Every time Shelbie is ill, I think she is going to die.' (She had a cold at the time of him saying this.) How hard that was to hear, and I couldn't reassure him that she wouldn't. I wouldn't lie to the children, otherwise when she did die, I would lose the trust my children had in me. I told him I felt the same and it was always OK to cry about it, and always OK to ask questions, too. The hospice was fabulous at supporting us all through this. I'm so glad we were there when it happened and they even extended our stay. I don't know how we would have managed otherwise. Kalan struggled for a long while afterwards, but he did settle again with lots of patience and understanding. Towards the end of the year, one of Shelbie's pals, Mitchell, who had had a tough year, died two weeks before Christmas. It was devastating seeing his whole family grieve and knowing the hurt that was to come. His eighteenth birthday had been coming up just a month later. I was with the family when he went and it tore me apart seeing his mum's hurt, but on a selfish level I realised that, one day, I would be doing that again. Your whole world changes forever, and I knew that family would never be the same again.

While Shelbie was in PICU the previous year, 2011, she'd received a Monmouthshire Pride Award. She was too poorly to go and receive it so Nick and I went on her behalf. It was hard not knowing at that time whether she would ever wake up to see the award, but she did. Then, months later, *Born To Be Different*, the TV programme which had been following Shelbie amongst others, won an AMI [Ability Media International] award which we took her to London for. You see, life does carry on and you have to adjust to it — quite a lot, sometimes — but those moments, precious little achievements, are massive, so I am so very proud of her for getting those awards, just for being the beautiful soul she is.

All families go through heartbreak and all go through moments of pride. I will always be proud of having the eight children I have, and have had, as they make mistakes along the way but also get it right at times and I love them every step of the way. I may not have had a high-flying career, but I am a mum and you will never convince me that I have missed out on anything in life, and that's because of them. I wouldn't change the Charlie or Shelbie path I was sent down for anything. I am who I am because of them, and they have made me stronger and more determined in life. I've never met a child who, the second she opens her eyes, is smiling and clapping as though she is happy to see another day. It's a shame we haven't all got that attitude. I know I certainly haven't. I never want to get out of bed, and I certainly don't hop out with a spring in my step, more a spring stuck in my back as I grumble and roll out! But if God had asked me in the beginning, would I rather have a child with special needs or without, I imagine my reaction would be without — not because I don't love Shelbie or Charlie just the way they were born, but because no parent wants to see their child struggle. And also, there are other people's attitudes and reactions to contend with. No one ever says, 'Wow, a kid with special needs, isn't it fab that you've been so blessed with such a special child.'

It's more, 'Oh dear…', or if they don't say it you just get "the look". Any child is special, any life is a blessing, but when you have a child with special needs you get more of an insight into what unconditional love is. I feel privileged that God thinks I'm up to the job. When Shelbs is in pain, I'd take that away in a heartbeat if I could, but her special needs are what makes her who she is. Bring that on any time!

When we went on stage to receive the AMI award, Patrick, the producer, said in his speech, 'Bringing up a child with special needs is not some marginal activity. It's normal and it's filled with hopes, fears and joys as any normal childhood. It's just that the challenges that these children face are bigger and more complex. The strength, commitment and love shown by the parents is a lesson for us all.'

The children have the same hopes and dreams as the rest of us, and they have to work harder to get them. But get them they do, and that's something we can all learn from.

You are

You are the most beautiful child I have ever met
Not just on the outside but most powerfully on the inside
You are so strong, so determined, so stubborn!

You let nothing hold you down
You love anybody that gives you chance
Whatever their misfortunes, whatever their attitude—
You're willing to love.

So many people underestimate you,
Don't look past your disabilities—
But for the ones that do,
They are blessed enough to get to know the real you.

You are a girl with so much love,
Have a wicked sense of humour,
Always willing to learn and try things
And are always happy.

You are also a beautiful star,
Enjoying life, loving socialising
Loving being the centre of attention
And loving your family dearly.

All these things make us so proud of you
For these are the things that make you so wonderful
So easy to love, so much pleasure to be around.

Never stop being you, Shelbs
Because you are truly amazing
And we love you so much it hurts sometimes,
But we'd have that pain every day if it means having you to wake up to.

Chapter Nine

Shelbie started having episodes of blood in her stoma and increased vomiting, containing blood, sometimes pure blood. She also had it coming out of her gastrostomy. She would have to be admitted, usually requiring a blood transfusion. She was also having periods of excruciating pain. We spoke with the children's palliative nurse, who we were familiar with and had started having more contact with her once Nick and I knew that there was some obvious deterioration starting to happen. We had a good run out of hospital (other than overnight stays for the transfusions) but these periods of pain were really upsetting us. Usually when something wasn't quite right with Shelbs, it might take a while but we would work out the problem. We were pretty sure it was her stomach hurting her but were never one hundred per cent convinced. She did often settle if I rubbed her stomach but I noticed more than anything that she would want you to lie with her. These episodes could go months apart from each other, but they still distressed her, and us too. Our palliative nurse went through a plan with us for analgesics, and Shelbie was having morphine alongside other drugs when the pain got really bad.

Despite all of this, Shelbie was still enjoying life to the maximum. She had already been down death slides with Daddy. The first time she did this she was about four years old. Nick wanted to throw her down on her own, but I protested that she would get hurt (although I think I was just a scaredy cat). I looked around and there she was flying down this death slide on her own, screeching with delight! While staying at Little Bridge one time, we took her surfing. As she loved water, you can imagine the joy she got from being in the sea on a surfboard with Daddy. And she looked damn cute in her wet suit. If we went to the fair she would spin around on the tea cups, and in Disneyland — which we were blessed to be able to visit with her four times — she went on every single ride except one. We took her on the *Pirates Of The Caribbean* ride, then realised there would be a massive splash of water and, as much as Shelbs loved water, she used to choke all the time by shoving her hand in her mouth and swallowing it. We always used to joke that she was doing her own lung wash-out. She had obviously had it too many times in PICU and felt brave enough to do her own so she would shove a load of water in, cough and often vomit, and then we would suction her and notice her chest was clear. She was very smart, you see? So, in this ride, my sister-in-law, Emma, had her hand completely covering Shelbie's face to protect her, although it looked in the picture as though she was smothering her. Nick also took her on the *Space Mountain* ride, where she decided halfway around the ride she would stop breathing. We had thought she would be OK for a little while so Nick had no O_2 on him. All he could say was, 'Kid, you're going to have to stay blue or start breathing until we get off this ride.' Thankfully she sorted herself out, but lesson learned. Maybe the ride was a bit fast and next time she was definitely taking O_2 on with her, but she was still smiling and screeching so despite that little "blip", shall we call it, she still enjoyed the ride.

Life was very fast-paced with Shelbs even on a "quiet" day. Everything to her was just about cramming it all in, so the other children got opportunities that some may never get. People used to tell them they were so lucky, and, yes, they were blessed to have these opportunities and these crazy fun times, but it came at a high price for them because they also had to not only watch the heartbreak going on in the family but often be very much a part of it. It's funny though, I don't regret them having that childhood because I believe they are who they are because of it. They may not see it now but one day they will all look back and realise their hearts and their compassion were moulded by their life with Shelbie.

Shelbie's biggest trick, and one that served her the longest, was her ability to pull her stoma bag off. We tried every type of bag, every adhesive to make it stick, a bandage that went round her whole middle so she couldn't get to it (apparently!) but there was nothing stopping her. She would pick and pick until it was at least leaking, then she would roll in it and wipe through the carpet, or worse (or best in her eyes), in bed. We would wake up in the mornings and either the smell itself would wake us or she would shout until we went into her room and, as we approached, we would pick up the "fragrance". It was awful, and certainly ensured you woke up quickly. The trick then was to try to work out where to start first. She would have it up the walls, across her bed, and she would be covered in poo, literally from head to foot. It would be in her hair, her ears, her finger nails but, worst of all, in her mouth, and then she would give this almighty smile and start blowing kisses. I used to say to her, 'For someone who apparently won't have food in your mouth, you look very comfortable with the poo in there.' She would just grin at me. If she wanted food that tasted that bad, she only ever had to give my cooking a try!

Another one of her tricks was to the detriment of the younger three children, and later her nieces too, in her role as big sister and aunty; she played the same trick on them all. When they started crawling, she would shuffle subtly towards a wall, so they would crawl closer to the wall to avoid her. Then, once she had them by the wall, she would put her feet either side of their body high up on the wall, trapping them. They couldn't move either side, and because she had her legs up high and would even lift up her bum to give just a little more height for her feet, they couldn't crawl over her either. The only option left open to them was to sit and cry and wait for assistance. And because Shelbie loved the sound of crying, especially babies crying, she would fold her arms and with a huge grin, give a little chuckle. It was very clever of Madam, but very mean too!

When Shelbie was fourteen, we decided to get her baptised. She couldn't talk verbally and tell me that's what she wanted but I felt confident enough that I knew her heart, and, anyway, Nick and I could communicate with Shelbie without words. It's something you learn when a child is non-verbal. You learn to communicate in a deep way that no other person can, and you can't explain it. There were aspects of understanding and communicating back from Shelbs as well so we had certain ways with her. The day was incredible. Shelbie was well for it, and it was important for us to do it. We felt that Shelbie was always public about what she had in her heart, and this public commitment was just Shelbie bringing people in to hear The Word that she believed in. I gave a testimony on her behalf but all I said was only ever what I believed Shelbie was saying or teaching me and others.

174

But a few months later she had an awful accident and her femur in her right leg was broken. Nick and I weren't looking after her when it happened, and, to this day, there are a lot of question marks around the event. More to the point, though, what we saw our child go through was horrific. At the hospital they gave Shelbie a nerve blocker so they could straighten her leg, as her knee was at the same level as her thigh. I had to walk out, feeling sick. Nick stayed with her and said it was the most horrendous thing he had ever seen and been through with her. She had a leg brace on and couldn't roll. They operated and put a metal plate in her leg but her leg was misshapen and never returned to how it was before, and as a result she had one side of her body shorter than the other. We were up with her night after night because she was in pain or uncomfortable. I was so angry for a long time afterwards because I felt it was something that could have been avoided and Shelbs really wouldn't hurt a fly. She had endured so much in her life, and at the time I felt, 'Why does she have to go through this on top of everything else?' I was very angry that this had happened, and I was also angry with God. 'Does she not go through enough? She never, ever complains. Yet just months after her public declaration to you, she goes through this.' But, of course, it served no one to be angry or to apportion blame. We had to move on and concentrate on how to help her reduce the pain. It took about two months before the pain seemed to bother her less and she slowly attempted to move. It took a lot of persuading and encouragement, and she was very cautious, but of course she got there because she was Shelbie. She wasn't angry, so we couldn't be either. In cold weather it hurt her more, but we learned how to get around these things and how to massage her leg when it was hurting.

After this came the half-marathon, the first year it had been run across the Severn Bridge. Nick and Paul had been out running a few times as they were doing it together but then Shelbie became ill and Nick's training regime went out the window. He ran it anyway with no training, but Shelbie was in hospital and so couldn't attend. I was a bit sad as Shelbie picks up on atmosphere so I felt she would have enjoyed the experience, as she had when Paul did the Cardiff marathon the previous year. She enjoyed the walking around to different points to cheer everyone on and she loved all the clapping and noise but it couldn't happen this time. Nick would have had Shelbie everywhere he went if he could, and he used to threaten to take her to work. He's a qualified electrician, but as well as electrics he also does general building, and he reckoned she would love all the banging and drilling. I'm sure she would have, actually, but I think he just loved being with her.

We were still having these bleeds though and it was getting harder and harder to get any IV access. Shelbie had had so many lines put in over the years that she had scar tissue everywhere and, besides, her veins had always been rubbish anyway. As a result, the metabolic team eventually decided the need to have permanent IV access outweighed the risks of infection, especially as they had also found that Shelbie had bone marrow failure and would need regular transfusions. So, when Shelbs was about fifteen she had a portacath inserted so we would have IV access at all times. Well, that was the idea, but seeing as this is all about Shelbie it didn't always work out. To be able to use the line it had to be accessed, and then blood drawn back from it, before you could give anything through it. Once Shelbie was handed over to the adult team at eighteen, she would only ever bleed back for one of the district nurses. I watched the other nurses as they accessed the port and they were doing it correctly but they couldn't get her to bleed back, and Nick and I trained to access and de-access too, but it wouldn't make a difference. She would often only cooperate for this one nurse in particular, Jules. But with the regular bleeds and Shelbie often presenting symptoms of her bloods being low (i.e. a lot more tired, but not in the same way as when she was hypoglycaemic) and bruising starting to re-occur, Shelbie was having blood transfusions pretty much monthly. She would sometimes go a bit longer, but that was the general time in between each transfusion: a month. As usual, though, when Shelbie's bloods had been topped up, she was full of life and happy. We would have a very noisy child who just loved being. As I've said before, there were times where I could see deterioration, but once the metabolic treatment started, we felt there had been a great improvement. She did, however, start getting hay fever. Would that child stop at nothing to build on her list of conditions? At one point we wondered if she was just working through the alphabet! With antihistamines, it was as controlled as it could be, but yet another drug…

When she was fifteen, she also became an aunt, which was another positive. We never thought we would be blessed to witness her becoming Aunty Shelbie. Rhys and his partner at the time had a little girl, Sophia. Then the following year, Courtney had a little girl too, Aria. Wow, this was so magical! I just never thought Shelbs would be around for such an event. A new life is so much a miracle and Shelbie became aunty to two beautiful babies.

One evening we were tidying up after putting Shelbie to bed when her sats monitor started alarming. Nothing unusual — if we hadn't given her, her sleeping drugs, she would play with her bells for a while and watch TV. She would get grizzly at times and if we put her in her room to play, she would perk up. I guess it's no different to any other teenager. They want their space and certainly don't want to hang out with Mum and Dad all the time. This was especially so near bedtime. She would grizzle so you thought she was ready for bed, then as you put her pyjamas on and have a wash she would perk up, so we would just let her play while we tidied up. Of course, she would always be on the monitor if we weren't with her, so it alarming wasn't unusual as she would kick around and set the alarms off. So, Nick and I both went into her, expecting her to be laughing at us, but she had sats in the single numbers and was gasping, which was something new and unfamiliar. We are used to the low sats but not this, so I called for an ambulance.

She was taken to Bristol Children's Hospital where she was well known and, when we got there, the PICU team were waiting in resus for us, although by this point, she wasn't gasping any longer. In fact, she was rolling around blowing raspberries! I'm glad the paramedics saw her as she had been so someone knew it was "real", but we still looked like frauds when we got there. Shelbie was kept in the high dependency unit (HDU) and then discharged the following morning with no more episodes. Huw Thomas just said it could be seizure related and if it happened again to give emergency anticonvulsants and ride it through.

We got home and that night the same thing happened again, which made me think that maybe it was a seizure because it wasn't unusual for Shelbie to fit more at night. We gave her paraldehyde, which was her rescue meds for seizures, and after a while it stopped but we weren't sure if it was the drug because that normally kicked in within minutes but this had taken fifteen to twenty minutes. As such I became less convinced it was seizure related, but she went to sleep and all was well for now.

Shelbie had respite nurses the following day. The qualified nurse was a regular but the health care assistant was new to Shelbs and it was her first shift. They had only been there about an hour or two when the qualified nurse called me and said, 'Shelbie is having difficulty breathing.' I went in and she was gasping again with dangerously low sats. She was doing like a rocking horse movement with her breathing and I didn't want to risk having to explain this again and doctors not realising just what was happening — it was very difficult to explain — so Nick filmed her. That sounds really awful but it proved so useful over the coming weeks. Meanwhile, this poor HCA had been subjected to Shelbie's antics from the start of her shift, and now the sicko father is filming his daughter gasping to breath. Poor girl must have been petrified! We never saw her again, and I often wonder whether she continued in that line of work or if Shelbie was enough to put her off for life. (She probably felt that a local supermarket job was looking quite tempting while all this was going on!) It wouldn't have been the first time Shelbie had scared people away. Over the years we had numerous qualified paediatric nurses who would come out to meet her or didn't even make it to the house — they would read the care plan and cancel the shift, because on paper Shelbs seemed scary — but the amount of nurses that said that once they had looked after her, although they were nervous when they'd read her care plan, they were glad they'd come because once you got to know her she wasn't at all scary and she had this fantastic personality that you'd want to be around. More than once we would have little messages in her medical notes thanking Shelbie for a fantastic shift and saying that they looked forward to coming back and looking after her again. It used to put a lump in my throat, but I didn't need telling how fantastic she was to be with. I was privileged to see that cheekiness every day.

So, we'd called for an ambulance and were taken to a closer hospital because of how unstable Madam's breathing was. She stopped gasping on the way but paramedics explained to the hospital staff what they had witnessed, and we also showed them the video and they did look a little concerned. One doctor came in and was asking us to go through what happened and pointed out that she'd stopped now. 'Yes, I know, thanks,' I was thinking.

Then Shelbie started doing it again, and so eventually she was moved to the HDU where she had another episode. But this time it didn't stop. She was gasping for hours and the nurses were taking it in turns to hold her head up for her to be able to get some breath in. The doctor wasn't rushing at all or even coming to her side, despite being sat in the ward with us. I was starting to get frustrated. My daughter had been gasping for a couple of hours, and she was getting tired now. I told him she needed support with her breathing, that he needed to do something before she went completely tits up — I think those were my words — and it ended up at the point of no return. He wasn't listening and he certainly wasn't doing a lot. I kept saying the same thing to him, and then I started asking him to ring Bristol PICU. He said he would speak to Cardiff, which made no sense as Cardiff didn't know her. I kept on and on but got nowhere until eventually a new doctor came on shift. He was brought up to date by us, and I explained that Shelbie was tired and probably needed ventilating now, and could she go to Bristol where they knew her. He told us he completely agreed that she needed ventilating and it made complete sense for the doctors that knew her to see her. Hallelujah. We were finally getting somewhere. The retrieval team from Bristol PICU came to get Shelbie, ventilated her, then took her back to Bristol. We explained all that had been happening and showed the doctors the video. I went in the ambulance with Shelbie to Bristol and Nick drove behind, while Paul and Emma who'd been with us all day, headed home. We waited in the parents' room for them to settle Shelbs, not realising that this would be the longest stay with Shelbie in PICU that we'd ever been though.

We didn't know that it would be the last time we would class this as Shelbs' second home. We would moan about doctors sometimes and how certain things were done, but it's not until you are faced with never doing this familiar routine again that you realise just how precious all those professionals were. Especially the long-term doctors. Dr Stanley had retired by this point, but Huw Thomas had been with us from the beginning and we trusted his judgement and support immensely. We, in effect, were going to be doing this alone now and at this point we didn't know any of this.

But here we were, back in PICU, with something very alien to us. This was all so different with Madam, not a typical chest infection or because of an operation: we were here for something totally new. Nick went back to get the children and I stayed at the hospital. The following day I was in the hospital hallway when I bumped into Shelbs' physio, Christina. She looked at me and said, 'She's not in, is she?'

I replied, 'Yep, in PICU I'm afraid.' She told me she would go in to see her. We still weren't really sure what was going on and I really struggled on this admission, maybe because I'd felt the deteriorations of late, but also because this time seemed different, medically.

After a few days they were hoping to extubate if Shelbs was ready but she wasn't bothering to take breaths when they tried getting her to breathe on her own. After a few hours she made some effort, but as usual it was always on her terms and when she was ready, not when they or we needed or wanted her to.

Three days after she'd been ventilated, they managed to extubate Shelbie. The following day, although Shelbs was doing well in herself, both her lungs were partially collapsed. Because we had done this so often and she had had so many X-rays we knew what was good for her and what was bad. They asked us in the other hospital to look at the X-rays and tell us if they were OK for her, as what an X-ray should look like for a typical person and one who suffered with their lungs or whatever might be was a totally different ball game. If you don't know that child, it is always better to ask Mum or Dad as they know their child's 'norm'. We kept ourselves well informed with everything, because we knew wherever Shelbs was, we would be with her so would know if something was different or not right. The physios and doctors at Bristol Children's Hospital did know Shelbs and her 'norms' but they would always keep us in the loop, so physio showed us her recent X-rays (which she was having daily) and they weren't looking too good. Just three days after being extubated Shelbie was put back onto ventilation as, medically, she was going back downhill. And although she went onto BiPAP, while all this was going on, Shelbie kept on with her cheekiness. Every time the physio put her on her side she just rolled onto her back, turned herself sideways (which was how she always laid in her bed at home) and stuck her feet over the side of the bed. It was a bit of a, 'No thanks, I'm comfier this way. I don't care how much you need me that way to work on me or help my breathing, I'm going this way and I'm staying this way!'

On quite a few occasions when Shelbie was gasping, her sats were doing stupid numbers. On one occasion the nurse said, after we'd got her breathing stable, 'I can't believe what I just saw. I've never seen sats of two before!' Well, no, because in theory she shouldn't be alive at that point.

There was another time when she had a gasp then a massive desat. I called for help as the nurse wasn't in the room at that point and in the end, we had countless doctors and nurses rushing in to get Shelbie — who had sats of nine — breathing. One of the doctors said he never would have believed it if he hadn't seen it for himself. I had been telling them for years that she could do single number saturations, but would get that look of, "Hmm, if you say so", or else they would say something like, 'No, if sats go below about twenty it's not a true reading'. It was always so frustrating, not being believed. I knew what I was looking for, and I knew how to read a trace. I was actually quite competent at this job, and had been doing it for a long time by now. Shelbie, of course, made her own feelings known. After they'd got her breathing once more and her sats were back up, all the medical staff stood back with a collective sigh of relief and a look of disbelief on their faces. Shelbs crossed her arms and surveyed everyone, and then blew raspberries at them as if nothing had happened!

James Frasier, one of the PICU doctors we had known for many years, came and spoke to me. 'Usually, after a week of being in, the child gets allocated a named consultant. She's been here nearly two weeks now so who do you want?'

I said, 'You.' We knew and very much trusted him. He may come across as a bit blunt to some people, especially if you don't know him, but he is one of the most trusted and capable consultants that I have ever come across — and we've come across quite a few, believe me. He said he wasn't able to take Shelbie on at the moment and neither could our second option, David Grant, (he had already asked him, knowing we would name him) so then I remembered Adrian Humphries who had been in and out quite a bit since Madam had been in. He hadn't always agreed with us on things, but that didn't matter. He always listened and I liked the fact he was honest with us if he felt there was a different approach, so James went off to ask him and that was it. Adrian was our PICU consultant for this stay, still working alongside Huw, who knew Shelbie best, and of course the physios.

Just after a week after going onto the BiPAP, doctors informed us that with the way Shelbie's breathing was, and with these gasping episodes, she probably wouldn't ever come off the ventilator. I felt gutted for her because although she didn't have to have the tube going down her throat, she was still going to be somewhat restricted — it would still be a big change for her and for the rest of us, come to that. But they did say they wouldn't know for definite until they had investigated. Ear, nose and throat doctors had come in to see what was going on with these "episodes" and thought there might be some kind of collapse in her airways. If this was the case, she would need a tracheostomy. This wasn't news to us, really. We had been warned fifteen years ago that this could be a possibility some day. I told the doctors what had been found all those years back and wondered if the tracheomalacia was causing a problem now. One of the doctors said she would have grown out of it by now, otherwise it would have caused problems much earlier on. I wasn't convinced as I knew how my daughter worked — the complete opposite of what was expected! The doctors checked her over and, after some kind of test, realised that it wasn't what they thought it was going to be — no, Shelbie, of course it wasn't, that would be way too easy! So it was decided that she would need to go to theatre under general anaesthetic for a proper investigation.

Nick and I wondered if, in fact, what she was having was some kind of periodic collapse and we did mention this to a few people who agreed that it might be. At this point we were still showing that "gasping" video to anyone who hadn't seen it. One morning, Adrian came in and said, 'I think she's having a periodic collapse of the airways somewhere.' YES! We definitely agreed on that one. I explained that we had felt the exact same thing for days. Shelbie was due for theatre the next day, after which we'd hopefully know more and find out whether she would have to stay on the ventilator forever.

In the meantime, and because it's Shelbie and she'd never let the grass grow underneath her feet, as they say, another problem was found. A scan had determined that her diaphragm wasn't working. The medical term for this is paradoxical movement, right hemidiaphragm — basically, her diaphragm wasn't moving up and down, left side and right side together as it should, but was moving up and down at opposite times, and as the diaphragm is the primary muscle that controls your breathing this causes a problem with breathing. The paradoxical movement causes the chest to move the opposite way to how it should. What else was there to say except her breathing was buggered! We knew this alone wasn't good. Goodness knows what they would find in theatre. We also knew this was something new as Huw said she'd had this scanned about three years before and there was no problem then. He couldn't understand what had caused it.

We didn't know if this was playing a big part in her breathing problems or just something else that was causing the main issue more complications, but they were sure now she certainly would never breathe on her own again. We were gutted, to say the least.

The following day was investigation day. When Shelbie came back from theatre, they said she still had tracheomalacia (oh, shocker… not!) and that she was looking quite different. She now had a big ventilating tube coming out of her nose. While in theatre they put a NPA (a nasopharayngeal airway) in and she was tolerating optiflow on it. Optiflow is a form of oxygen, if you like, but delivering a higher amount without drying the airway out. It warms and humidifies high flow oxygen or air via nasal cannulas, so it's another form of NIV, but a lot less invasive than the face mask. It was felt that she was probably having periodic collapses, but it still wasn't clear why.

Adrian came into her room one afternoon and asked to speak to us somewhere else. This is never good. Although when Shelbie was younger, we would sometimes ask to talk elsewhere as she had that understanding and we didn't want to scare her with things, we would generally just talk outside of her door, but Adrian started walking across the ward. I said to Nick, 'Oh crap, as long as he doesn't take us to the parents' quiet room,' which is where we've often had bad news given to us, as have other families. Yep, that's where he headed. I turned to Adrian and said, 'This isn't good then, is it? This is where all the bad news is delivered.'

'Not at all, it's just quieter in here,' he responded. I wasn't convinced. No one goes in there, because it's the dreaded Bad News Room. I might look stupid, but I'm actually not!

We sat and waited for Huw to join us. It's definitely not like feeling positive vibes when two of them want to talk to you. Huw explained about the findings of her diaphragm and this new NPA. After a lengthy discussion and quite a few tears, and after going home and talking to all the children together, it was decided that if Shelbie couldn't manage with just having the NPA in and O_2 and not the BiPAP, then it was time to let her go. We were going to give her another week to see how she did, but we didn't want her to struggle any more. And she was struggling. It wasn't fair on her. She did manage well on the optiflow with her airway in for the next week, but had a bad left lung collapse so was on the BiPAP more. It felt like a little step forward and two back, but she was very, very happy in herself. In fact, she was bouncing off the walls as though she had just had to suss a new way of breathing on a different machine and once she had worked it out she was ready to go again. I never got my head around how she just went for it, how she always found a way around things. One massive plus was that, since having the airway in, there were no more gasping episodes at all.

The doctors had obviously seen that change in her as they told us she was definitely going the right way and they were pleased with her progress. They reckoned it could take six to twelve months to get her home, but Shelbie had decided that in fact we were going to go home on ventilation and that was that. She made the decision in her attitude, showing us, 'Look, it's OK, Mum and Dad, I'll just do it this way now, and we'll be fine.' So we followed her lead and started planning for her to come home. She did, in fact, need times on the BiPAP, but whatever, Shelbs, we've nothing else to do, let's just train for that too, shall we!

The vent didn't stop her at all, she just worked around it. Adrian was hoping she could come home on CPAP, as it was a lot less of a headache with regards to Shelbie's home care package and the training for it, but

Shelbie was just getting too tired. Her breathing pattern had changed and it wasn't as good as it had been, and there were times where she really struggled and would go very clammy so needed a complete break with the breathing, and that's what the BiPAP did for her. After an hour's break she would have the energy to start all over again, so, in her eyes, all was good. And what she thought and how she felt was all that mattered.

Six weeks into her admission we had a multi-disciplinary team meeting, where all the professionals involved could come together and work out a plan of what would happen next, and also be updated as to where we were now, following the recent events. Shelbie was coming up to seventeen, so the adult team came to the meeting as well so they were well informed. At the meeting, Dr Thomas said how in the past week or so, Shelbie was demonstrating her usual happy, active character traits again. They were going to try and wean her off the NPA, as it posed issues for longer term care at home, but Nick and I weren't keen, thinking along the lines of "if it ain't broke, don't try to fix it". For whatever reason, Shelbie wasn't having the episodes since the NPA, and when you attempted to remove it, even just to clean it or change it, she would go blue and get herself in a state. It may well have been psychological, I don't know, but physio trained us to maintain it and change it, so we didn't see it as an issue. The hospital said it was very unusual for a child to have an NPA in the community, which made me feel like we would certainly be going home with it then, because Shelbie likes to do the unusual.

We talked about the nursing support we would need at home. Huw wanted us to have seven nights a week as he said we would have to stay up with her all night, because she would be ventilated. I explained that we were aware that Shelbie's prognosis was shorter now because of all of these new breathing problems. Huw commented, 'I'm not sure how Shelbie is so, so well at the moment, she is like a ball bouncing off the walls in her room, but it won't last. We are sending her home on the ventilator to hopefully increase the time she has with you, but we are talking months, not years.'

Adrian explained that there would be risks to further full ventilation and it wouldn't be beneficial to do more than BiPAP, but if she got ill because she was a vent patient she would always have to go to ICU or HDU, and because Shelbie was nearly seventeen, she would need to start using adult hospitals. We talked to Adrian and Huw alone and, with taking all this into account, it was decided that there would be no more active treatment for Shelbie, from now on it would just be palliative care. The time we had left we were going to make the most of, with the right support.

Poem

Written while Shelbie was in PICU

You've changed our world:
When you arrived so delicate and small
I knew you were special, you'd captured my heart already
Each day we've woken up together the love's grown stronger
I've learned so much along the way, grown so much because of you.
The years have gone by and not one day has been wasted
Every smile and every tear has been for a reason
And there's been so much laughter — it's outweighed the heartache.

I've never met anyone before who has such a lot to say, yet can't talk
Who smiles so beautifully, making the darkest days bright
Whose eyes sparkle, with life shining out of them
Every second is a second to be had — making everything you do count
for something
Making the simplest of things the biggest lessons we'll learn.

Who could go through their life being that blessed?
Well, it's us, precious.
Who could ever think they weren't given the best deal?
Certainly not us.
We feel so blessed that we were chosen to guide you — but we certainly
never taught you — you taught us
The most precious lessons we could ever learn are that of
Love, acceptance, tolerance, patience, strength
And never to assume, judge, hurt, refuse or deny.

Thank you for all you give us, all you teach us,
The love you continue to share with us.
We love you now, tomorrow and always
You're beautiful on the outside and even more beautiful on the inside.

Chapter Ten

The next month or so was spent planning to go home, making sure there would be a care package in place when we got there together with all the support we needed, but sadly we didn't have the best input in general from our children's team so nothing was moving particularly fast. Nick was getting frustrated. He just wanted Shelbie home, where she should be, especially as in herself she was the best she'd been in a long while. We had passed the vent training, so it was literally just a matter of making sure the right people were ready when we left.

In the end, Nick told Huw he was taking Shelbie before her birthday, which was the following month. It wasn't going to be possible to get any kind of package in place in that short space of time so Nick said we would take her home without a package and do it ourselves. A friend who had looked after her son at home told us not to do it. 'I get you want to take her home but you will be on your knees within weeks. It is so tiring. Trust me I've been there.'

Huw also said to us, 'You won't be able to manage it. Shelbie's care is a lot more intense than it was before, you won't physically cope.' But we wouldn't listen. Our worry was that she would die in hospital waiting to get home. We could have her out for day release but that in itself was draining, going back and forwards to hospital for what could be up to a year, which we'd been told was the more realistic timescale. Also, financially we wouldn't cope. Another year of driving in and out of hospital. Of course, we would have done it if we had had to, but being brutally honest, it was a worry, especially as we had made the decision for Nick to take time out of work so he could have those last few months with Shelbie. No amount of money in the world was worth missing her life, but I don't think people consider the financial impact. The number of people we met over the years and especially at Ronald McDonald House who'd struggled financially. It's OK if you have someone to cook your meals daily, but the reality is that not many parents, if any, do have that option. You could take a packed lunch to hospital every day but it's enough to try to get out of bed in the morning, and as soon as you are up you just want to be there with them. And if you've stayed in you have no choice but to buy meals each day anyway. Then, by the time you leave the hospital at night you have no energy to cook and it's usually too late for the little ones anyway, they've had to be fed. Add in the petrol day in, day out, buying little gifts to try to distract them, or just because you love them. The drop in wages when you take time off from work and don't get paid… It's difficult: you have to be with your child and family, but you also can't live on fresh air. You are torn both ways. It's an impossible decision for whichever parent has to make it, more often than not it's Daddy. With that drop in wages, you have to decide whether to use what money you do have to pay for petrol and food, and often your phone bill will take priority — firstly because you want to let family know what's happening, but just as importantly it is vital to stay connected for yourself and your own sanity. And, of course, the hospital needs to be able to contact you. So you get behind on the mortgage, because you just don't have enough money to spread all the ways it needs to go. It is an added stress you really don't need but, bottom line, you can only think of getting to and being with that child.

After about a month, with Nick still pushing to get Shelbie home and one of the physios laughing at him, telling him it was a bit of a dream if Nick thought she would be home for her birthday ('Maybe Easter but not her birthday'), we walked out of the door to take our princess home, with all of her new medical equipment in tow. We had to stop several times on the way home as Shelbie required very regular suctioning. We had gone from being suctioned three to four times a day when she was poorly to at least every half an hour day and night all the time. It was tiring enough in hospital, let alone when we got home and had to run a household.

While waiting to bring her home we had spent some days decorating and blitzing the house, especially Shelbs' room, so we didn't have to think about it when she got back. We had decided that while one dealt with Shelbs, the other would manage the other kids, as we did in hospital, but it wasn't that easy. There were times Shelbie took both of us which we hadn't taken into consideration — there was always a nurse on hand in hospital but now at home we didn't even have a nurse for a few hours each day. We were spending entire days and nights in her room. The pair of us stayed awake between us for just over a week, grabbing an hour here and there before we realised it was unrealistic. This had become a form of torture. So, we put a mini sofa bed in her room and both slept in there. A few people asked us why we don't take it in turns. As much as we don't hold any grudges and feel it a privilege to look after Shelbie, we were only human and had given up a lot to be with her — but why should we not be a married couple as well. We should be allowed to go to bed together, plus, if anything did happen, what if the other person wasn't there or couldn't be woken. It wasn't worth the risk to us so, while it might not have been ideal, we both stayed in with her. But after two weeks of being home we realised what a mistake we'd made. (Or, to put it another way, 'Oh, crap, what have we done?') We were on our knees with tiredness, as we had been warned, but it was too late. We had committed to it, so we just had to drag ourselves until a few months passed and we finally had nurses to help out.

We were still suctioning Shelbie very regularly but it did seem to lessen and she was as happy as ever, and once she got the nurses back, we put her into school part-time again, not because we wanted to — we would have kept her at home with us so we didn't miss a moment with her — but because she needed it. She loved school for a start, but also, we knew she needed to live and not just exist, and that for her meant being in school with her friends. I realised that when we brought her home and not long after we went to visit her friends just before Christmas. They were ecstatic to see her, but more importantly, she was happy to see them too and we knew we had to do all we could to give her that time back, however short it might be.

Shelbie was actually doing well. She had got a new rhythm of breathing sussed and she had breaks throughout the day on her ventilator, and at night. She would get to about four or five o'clock in the afternoon and you could see she was getting tired, her breathing pattern would change and she would often need the vent quite early, but otherwise this was OK for now. Just weeks after going back to school, both we and the nurses noticed that Shelbie wasn't really using her left arm and leg and had started dribbling from the left side of her mouth. We were due to go to Little Bridge House, so once we were there, I raised it with one of the doctors who knew Shelbie. He checked her over and, after the examination, took us to the small lounge to talk. Again, just like the parents' quiet room in PICU we knew this was never good, although this room was used for just sitting in to chill as well.

He confirmed what we had already suspected. She had had a stroke. He said that with the way the symptoms were presenting it was likely she had a brain tumour. The only way to determine this was with a scan, but Shelbs would have to have a general anaesthetic and we weren't prepared to take that risk just so that we could tick a box to confirm that's what it was. Her treatment wasn't going to change, so we just carried on, but in the knowledge now that there was something else probably killing her.

She had about five chest infections that winter, and a few of the infections required IV antibiotics. As I wasn't keen on Shelbie going into a new hospital and the adult district nurses were now having more to do with Shelbie, I asked if she could have IVs at home, and it was agreed. But then we found out that the nurses were a bit short staffed over the weekend and couldn't get out to do her drugs, so as she had already started them at this point, I told them to train me up to do IV drugs. I was adamant she wasn't being admitted. Nick knew how to access her IV port and I knew how to de-access it, so they trained me to do the in-between bit. Once we realised that Shelbie was on home ventilation and could never be fully ventilated again, and I could now do the IVs too, there was no reason for her to ever go to hospital again so I told her she would never have to because whatever needed doing Mummy and Daddy would do it for her. She had spent seventeen years going back and forth to hospital, so her remaining time was going to be hospital-free. While in some ways it was a lot of pressure doing it all, and we often felt very alone (especially not having Huw Thomas to fall back on any more), it was also a relief. Nick was still off work, so nursery and school runs were OK, and whatever we needed to do we could just work around at home when she was ill. Meetings, everything, had to be done at our house, but it was all manageable. And we didn't have to worry about dragging the kids into hospital, and them then being stuck inside all day, as they could just carry on in their home as before, whether she was ill or not.

I spent a long while when she came home worrying, always wondering when we went out or went away if that was the last time we would do that with her, or would she see that (or them) again? I was struggling more than I had realised, and it made me not very nice to be around. Plus, I think the exhaustion didn't help. One day I was praying for strength, patience and peace. I realised I hadn't been living, I hadn't enjoyed the time with Shelbie because I was too scared, focusing too much on her dying. I realised then that I had to start living. I was doing the thing Shelbs was the opposite of: I was just existing. What was the point of fighting to get her home so quickly when I wasn't making those times count? So from then on, whatever was thrown at us, we tried to start really living, making the best of whatever moments we had.

Shelbie's breathing started improving and she was managing some days off the vent altogether, just using it at night and that was more because we were administering her sleeping drugs, so we put her on it so as not to disturb her, rather than it being because she needed it. Despite the stroke, she still kept trying, and she still had that infectious smile. But she could no longer roll over, and she had stopped sucking her thumb. She couldn't blow raspberries any more, or say Mamma, or blow kisses and she was a lot quieter than she used to be. I hated that stroke with a vengeance. I would get so angry at what it had robbed her of. The breathing, yes, we understood that taking her — she had always suffered with her breathing in one way or another so that seemed inevitable. But a stroke? Why? She was dying anyway, so why that? Shelbs didn't have that attitude though. She just plodded along, not worrying about what she couldn't do, but making the most of what she still could do. I wasn't getting any answer, I never would, so I had to follow her lead and just make the most of an awful situation. We still went camping several times that year and that was important because that was her love.

About the same time as the stroke, Sophia, Rhys' daughter, came to live with us. We started training as foster carers in order to keep her with us until she was eighteen. That was difficult, not the training as such, but because when we had to go to court ten months later to get it all finalised the judge was awful to us, questioning our ability and whether we were protecting Sophia. He decided to adjourn court for the day to decide whether we got to keep her or not. The most heartbreaking thing was that we were sent home the day before Shelbie's eighteenth birthday, and the judge didn't inform us of his decision until four p.m. on Shelbs' birthday itself. We were so drained by then that we were too tired to celebrate. We went out a few days later with Shelbie's friends, William and Lewis, and had a fantastic time, and in that respect, Shelbie had the best birthday possible but that time, that one particular day, can never be got back. We missed celebrating her actual birthday and we can never change that, and that does make me sad. We never thought in our wildest dreams that she would reach that day and yet then it was taken from us anyway. It wasn't even because we had Shelbie that there was a question mark over our ability. She was, in fact, our saving grace. It was because the care we had proved to have given her made him realise that we would also protect this precious little life too, so with regards to Sophia, all went well in the end. She had been with us for ten months at this point and I couldn't imagine not having her in our lives.

For about eight years I had suffered a lot of pain and fatigue and was finally diagnosed with fibromyalgia. The rheumatologist tried various medications which took the edge off but I started looking into alternative medicine after a particularly bad flare-up. I couldn't even get off of the sofa to go to the toilet, and it had got so bad that I was taking over an hour to get out of bed. I couldn't get up to Shelbie when she alarmed, and that really scared me. So I went gluten-free and tried some herbal remedies and, although I do get the odd flare-ups and the pain is constantly there, I can ignore it. It is the best it has ever been, but it did worry me that I wouldn't be able to see to Shelbs if she was struggling, which meant it often fell on Nick which wasn't fair. I just couldn't do anything about it. I don't know if my body had just given up after so many years of lifting Shelbs and not getting the rest I needed, but I certainly suffered for it.

Christmas 2016 was pretty much the same as ever. By now Shelbie had now done a year from PICU after being told we only had months and, while she was ill throughout, we still carried on and had a fantastic time in between these bouts of bad days. And Shelbs was now in school full-time despite having chest infections a lot more often.

One thing I did pray for was for Shelbie to see snow one more time and this winter it snowed heavily. It was so beautiful. I didn't take her out in it like we used to but we sat by the front door just watching the snow come down. We did go out on the drive for just a few seconds so she could feel it coming down, but it was so magical, it's something we just take for granted that we'll see again, but for Shelbie we just weren't sure. In fact, she was lucky because she saw it this year and the year after too, which I certainly hadn't expected.

Over the years we had bad days where Shelbie would appear in pain and a lot of the time it was down to the migraines she suffered. We would put her in her bedroom in darkness and silence, give her a sleeping drug and analgesics and tiptoe around until she felt better. This generally would work. She also suffered dystonia (uncontrolled muscle movements) and this would also cause her a lot of pain and distress so we had to give her a strong sedative to help her totally relax. This obviously resulted in her sleeping for a long time when she was sedated, but it was necessary. If she was only suffering with it mildly, we could often distract her and massage it, and then sometimes it would pass.

But Shelbie started suffering a lot of pain again, and it seemed different to us to the migraines or dystonia. We often wondered if it was more due to the tumour that she may have, rather than the migraines, the dystonia or her stomach. After the major operation on her bowel, Shelbie didn't tolerate sitting for too long. We tried different cushions and seating but nothing worked, so as much as possible she would be left rolling around the floor, which she much preferred anyway. But everything we had tried to relieve the pain for all of this wasn't working. We were having regular contact with the palliative team under the adult services, which was absolutely fantastic, and we saw the palliative consultant every month; she would come to the home so we didn't have to drag Shelbie out and so it didn't matter if she was ill. This team and the district nurses were our strength, and I don't know how we would have got through without them. Everyone had told me, through Shelbie's teens, 'Oh, you wait until you go over to adult care, it's awful, you won't appreciate what you've got now until you change over.' But that wasn't our experience at all. It was all extremely positive.

There was one thing that we did struggle with, however, and that was the lack of listening and understanding. We'd gone eighteen years with telling professionals how things were done, and what worked for our daughter. The doctors used to tell us we were the experts and a lot of them followed our lead because we spent every day with her and that qualified us to take charge. That's not dismissing the care and support that most of the doctors gave, especially Huw Thomas, we would never have had the confidence if it hadn't been for him not only showing us the way but also being prepared to listen to our side too. But now, all of a sudden, there were managers, nurses and doctors telling us how it was going to be done or having meetings either without us (or totally ignoring the fact that we were in attendance), making decisions about our daughter. We literally felt invisible when we gave our input. Not only was this downright rude and inexcusable, but it was also a very dangerous approach. Our thoughts were along the lines of, 'You've come into my daughter's life eighteen years in and, from a few notes, have presumed to not only know her, but to know what is best for her.' It was very scary. In effect, because of her age we had no say in what was happening to her. This is fundamentally wrong and something in the system needs to be addressed to change that. It's a massive flaw in the system, and one day if it is not dealt with it is going to cost a "child" their life. Decisions appear to be made on what the professionals know from their books — yet anyone with a special child knows there is no such book. The "book" they should be reading from and following has a simple title: *Ask Mum And Dad*. They should take your every word on what you are saying for your child, especially if the evidence shows you have been doing all of this successfully for eighteen years already. That should be enough to cover them when following your lead and advice rather than assuming that they know best.

The palliative team were very quick to respond when we rang them to say Shelbie was in pain. Shelbie would very often choose to be ill on a Friday evening and anyone who does this journey knows that no one is around on a weekend — no one who knows your child, at least. That you could guarantee. I often wonder if Shelbie did it to see me sweat all weekend, chasing around trying to find answers. It's the kind of thing she would find funny! But the palliative team gave us emergency numbers and made sure they were always contactable at "inconvenient" times, to lessen the worry for us. We tried a lot of different analgesics and sedatives and Shelbie was often on regular morphine, but some days none of this was enough and we just had to sit and watch her for days until it passed. Our GP said it could just be a result of her deteriorating, but whatever it was, it was a killer to witness.

One weekend was especially bad. We were supposed to be going out but she was in so much pain that Nick took the children out and I stayed in with her. I laid down with her, cwtching up, and she would sleep from exhaustion intermittently, but otherwise she was sobbing. I sat next to her and prayed over her, then sang to her. She loved me singing two songs in particular: 'Father's Eyes' by Amy Grant and 'Amazing Grace'. She would want me to sing over and over and if she was ill or having bloods done it was these two songs that could stop the tears. I used to dread it in hospital, she would look at me as if to say, please sing, Mum and I would think, 'Seriously, with the doctor and nurse here?' But I did it as I was singing for her, not them. I sat singing to her and even got half a smile, but you could see the effort she had to make to raise that smile. I sat crying with her and told her that she didn't have to keep fighting; if she was tired, she could go and we would understand. I explained that Daddy would find it hard to ever say the words, but she didn't need to worry, I would look after her, Daddy would understand and would never want to see her in pain. She absolutely sobbed and, in that moment, I realised that she wasn't crying because she was upset by what I was saying, thinking I didn't want her any more. She was crying because she knew she had had enough, but just didn't want to leave us. I genuinely think that's what was taking her so long. I often said to Nick, 'What is she waiting for? Is she waiting for someone or something?' I believe she just felt torn. She didn't want to be without her family, but she was also tired from the pain and the struggle.

I had decided to go to college to do an access to nursing course. I passed maths and English and started just a few weeks before this episode. I had also trained with Homestart, to go into families who were struggling for various reasons and just offer support and I had the first family I was due to start with.

This weekend passed, but it wasn't too long before we had another bad day, and it was the worst we had seen her (other than when she was in PICU, where generally there was an explanation). We managed to get through the weekend, then our GP came out and he too said this was the worst he had seen her. I asked if this could be the end and he agreed that yes, it could be. It was September 2018. Shelbie was coming up to her nineteenth birthday as the GP made arrangements for us to travel to Little Bridge House for end-of-life care, the very day I was due to start with Homestart, which was understandably cancelled.

The following day we set off to Little Bridge House, for end-of-life care. This wasn't going to be an easy task. The night before we headed off, the district nurse came out to give Shelbie diamorphine to help her feel relaxed and not so agitated. The plan was if Shelbie was ready, her little body would just take the drug along with other drugs like midazolam, anti-sickness meds etc., and these drugs all together would help her feel completely chilled and out of it. (These are what I call her end-of-life drugs.) Well, of course, because this is Shelbie it wasn't going to go like that. The nurse gave the injection and then left. About twenty minutes later Shelbie desaturated into single figures, gasping for breath — we hadn't seen any gasping like this since she left PICU. It was horrific to witness. Mike, my cousin, was with us for support, and it certainly wasn't fair for him to see this or for Shelbie to meet the end in this way. There was no way she was going like this: no one should have to die looking so scared and panicked.

Nick and I were bagging Shelbie and willing her to live. She had six of these episodes in the space of half an hour. We finally calmed her and got her breathing stable again. The nurse was due out a few hours later to give the midazolam, but we rang her and said she wasn't being given anything else until she got to Little Bridge House. We had cancelled the night nurse because we felt if these were her last days then we wanted to be with her, so I was scared now she was going to die in the night. It seems silly saving her, doesn't it, when we were going to a hospice for end of life, but I could not — would not — allow her to die in such an uncontrolled dramatic way. I just couldn't. Everything in me just made me automatically jump in to save her, because that was what my brain had been programmed to do for so many years. During those days of not really knowing how to help her, we had started giving Shelbs promethazine regularly. She would have it as she needed it for sleeping, but I guessed as it was a sedative it might help her. We were told by the GP it was good for headaches, so if her head had been causing her trouble it should help. To be honest, though, I hadn't given it as an educated guess — I was just desperate and had tried everything else.

We made it to the following day. We had district nurses, a palliative nurse and consultant and GPs in and out of the house all day. They wanted to ensure Shelbie was stable enough to make the journey down to Little Bridge House which was a good two-hour drive. They wanted her to go by ambulance, but we argued that she wasn't going in the ambulance and dying alone and, besides, we had to drive both cars so that we could take all the children anyway so it was impossible for one of us to be in the ambulance. And, anyway, even if only one of us needed to drive how do you decide who goes with her? Mummy, who brought her into this world? Or Daddy, who was her hero? How do you decide? So we were willing to take the risk of driving her. In the professionals' defence it wasn't Shelbie's regular nurse, consultant and GP — sod's law dictated that they were all on leave that week.

The GP then helpfully suggested that if we insisted on trying to take her ourselves, she could call the police to stop us removing her. It had already been agreed that Shelbie was stable enough for the journey, so there was no issue really, but it is scary thinking that someone else could call the shots like that for your child (whatever the age they're still your child, your baby). Who is anyone, especially someone who had never even met either Shelbie or us, to decide what is best for our child? It really threw me at the time.

It was finally agreed that Shelbie could travel down with us. She went in Daddy's car with Mummy right behind. We had been warned of the risks that she could die during the journey but, thank you God, she didn't. It took me all day to pack all of our stuff. Yes, there were people in and out of the house all day, but perhaps more importantly it took so long because I just couldn't bring myself to do it. My mind was on overdrive, thinking that this would be the last time I'd have to pack for this journey. This time I would have to take additional stuff like her funeral plan book and her school uniform that she would wear once she'd died. It was gut-twisting, but we did it. The journey wasn't at all straightforward. Nick had to stop several times to suction Shelbs and it took over three hours to get there. It's by the grace of God that Nick and I managed to focus enough to arrive safely. Once there, and once settled in, they started Shelbie on regular oramorph as this often helps with breathing, so she said. We had never been told this before, and there were plenty of times that this information would have been useful, but we knew now. Shelbie was taking short breaths, and the morphine in the drug sometimes relaxes the body enough to take in a proper breath.

We'd already called family and close friends before we'd left. Annmarie, my good friend from *Born To Be Different* and whose daughter had been a bridesmaid, drove all the way down from Essex without us knowing, just to say her goodbyes. There was a couple we were friendly with, Gareth and Zoë, who had two poorly children, and we'd met them five or so years before at Little Bridge House and we'd started booking stays there together. (They'd actually been in PICU at the same time as us and had been a massive support.) It turned out that they were already there for respite, which was quite a relief. They were really the only people who knew where we were at. They would sit with us in the evenings once their boys and Shelbs were settled, and we would talk and cry and laugh together. Oh, we so needed that laughter, and we always had a great time when we were together. And being tired meant that we would laugh at the silliest things but we didn't care, we just needed to let it out!

Once we'd arrived at Little Bridge House and got Shelbie settled, we had a talk with the managers, Mandi and Tracy. They said they wouldn't do anything for twenty-four hours, as they wanted to observe Shelbs and see where we were at. Tracy, who we have known for years, thought it was the end. 'But how long this end will be, I don't know.' I felt she was absolutely right. End of life doesn't necessarily mean days. It could be weeks, or even months. Sometimes people bounce back for a bit, even look better than they've done for quite a while, but it's pretty much the calm before the storm. They have this little high before they completely plummet. So we played it by ear for days and Dr Bruce, who knew her well, kept a close eye on things. One day he came in and surprised us.

'I'm not sure this is the end, you know,' he said. 'Not right now.' And he was right. Just about five or so days after we'd arrived at Little Bridge House Shelbie was in the jacuzzi with Nick.

This was fantastic. Of course, it was. But it didn't mean she was fixed. It just meant we had slightly longer. I wondered what this was doing to the other children. How many more times did they have to do this and have their emotions pushed to the edge? I thought they would get to a point of never believing she'd go, and then that would be harder for them. (And I think, from Shelbie's point of view, she just didn't know how to let go. She had spent her whole life fighting to be with us, so when she got ill it was instinct just to keep fighting. She literally knew no other way.) It certainly did affect them all, there can be no doubt about that, but they were glad she was coming home. For me, though, I knew this definitely was the beginning of the end. It would be months at the most. I had in my head that her birthday and Christmas would almost certainly be her last.

At least we didn't do this all alone, as Margarita and her partner, Jane, also came to be with us at Little Bridge House so we had friends from home by our side, too. We stayed there for a couple of weeks then went home, having agreed that as soon as Shelbie started deteriorating again, we would go straight back down. In actual fact, we were there a few weeks later as Shelbie was ill with a chest infection and by this point, I think we were starting to struggle. Then, weeks before Shelbs' nineteenth birthday, we went down again for a planned respite break that we had booked in with Gareth and Zoë and their family. We had an awesome time as usual — lots more tired silly giggles, but so worth it. We didn't have to explain how we felt because they already knew. One of their boys was on the palliative pathway too, and they have two other children, so they totally got our family. I didn't know it at the time, but this was to be the last visit with them at Little Bridge House. I always looked forward to our times together there and it would be so strange not to go any more.

After this visit Shelbie had her bloods checked and they were the best they had been in a while, so we were looking at getting her back into school. Only part-time now as she did seem to be getting tired more easily, but as she still loved school it was only right for her. We took her in to see her school friends and it was very emotional. To think that we never thought she would step foot in there again just a few months back.

Shelbie had always been famous for her low sats and lack of breathing, but something else we noticed now was how hard it was becoming to get her breathing. Her sats were more often dropping into single figures and it was taking a lot longer to get her breathing, but also it was a lot harder. We were having to bang on her chest sometimes and shake her little body to get any breaths despite bagging her, and my gut was telling me more and more how much we were watching her slip away.

Another thing that was becoming problematic were the internal bleeds. These were becoming more frequent and seemed to be larger and last longer, but one funny thing was, that at one point Shelbs was having transfusions and needing them monthly, but since PICU hadn't needed a single transfusion despite checking her bloods regularly, especially after a bleed. This made no sense — she had bone marrow failure: it can't just suddenly fix itself. Having said that, though, she managed to come off the thyroxine years before. When you have hypothyroidism, you have the medication for life, yet she had been on it for about fifteen years and then managed to come off it, so although none of it made sense, I think it's just how Madam worked.

These bleeds, I feel, were just another indicator of everything starting to shut down, along with often having blue feet for no apparent reason. These were all signs and I knew it. Bizarre though, isn't it, that at a time when things were getting worse, when we came out of PICU Shelbie was having to use the nebuliser seven times a day, with extra saline when needed, but now she was down to three a day. She just never failed to surprise me and prove that there was no manual for her. Doctors did say that anything that a medical professional is taught about how certain things work in the body she managed somehow to change or contradict, which made a stranger caring for her even harder, but this is what made Shelbie Eloise who she was. This is the person she had become and people just loved her for it.

We had been really blessed and that summer went to see *Peppa Pig* at Cattle Country Farm Park in Berkeley, Gloucestershire, with Gareth, Zoë and our children. We were still trying to build as many memories as we could. We were also sent one last time to Disneyland by a charity called Magic Moments and that was so true — these were going to be some of our last moments. On the final day, Shelbie had the biggest bleed she'd ever had, losing over a litre of blood. We gave extra fluids and guessed we were driving home that night so we would just persevere. Besides, by the colour of her, no hospital would have let her out: she was blue. We put her on O_2 and just prayed our way through the day. We figured if she died on the way home, we would just have to deal with it then. We got home in the early hours of Shelbie's birthday, so yet another birthday ill. Nothing overly unusual there!

A month later came Christmas, and for the first time ever, Shelbie was really well. She had an absolutely fantastic day at home. We all did. She was smiley and alert and just seemed to enjoy everything about Christmas Day. We have some gorgeous pictures of her smiling. It was just the best. And we were all together, even the older children, (and Courtney was expecting a baby, too) and things, for now, were going smoothly. Shelbie wasn't able to go back to school because the nurses looking after her had found work elsewhere when she went to Little Bridge House for end of life, but Nick was taking her in each week for her hydrotherapy sessions, and as long as she had water, life was good in her eyes. While she was off school, Nick and I were also taking her to stay at Whitemead, a forest park in Lydney, in the Forest of Dean, where she could go swimming. This seemed to be enough for her. She was slowing down so was now happy with just a few activities in the week.

The new year rolled around and the adults' team managed to find Shelbie some new nurses. These were ICU nurses, and I can't begin to explain the relief with having such qualified people. But it was necessary, and it was right; it was what Shelbie needed and deserved. If she had a desat, they wouldn't panic, they would just keep an eye on her and in turn she wouldn't panic and could usually sort it out for herself. But if she couldn't, they dealt with her with such professionalism. It was so refreshing and it meant she could go back to school once we were all happy that the nurses were on top of all her diagnoses.

It was about this time… Well, we'd decided that whatever came our way we would face it, but the reality was we needed to plan ahead a bit, so I decided to get a job at Shelbie's school as a carer. I could honestly say that I had plenty of experience, and I got put in a class with a teacher that used to have Shelbs years ago. It was nice to go in as Vicki, but once the staff knew who I was, I was more Shelbie's mum than Vicki. But, you know, that's OK. I am so proud to be known as 'Shelbie's mum'. I thoroughly enjoyed working there and the staff couldn't have been more helpful and more welcoming. I was so lucky and loved what I was doing. Once Shelbs was back in school, Nick would drop her off, as I had already left for work (I was based at the primary site and of course she was in secondary school) and then after work I would drive to the secondary site and pick her up. It worked well. In fact, things were as good as they were going to get.

From the September of Shelbie getting ill I had deferred my college course for a year. I also knew we had to start planning for her funeral. It's not a nice thing to talk about, or even think about, but it was reality and we had to face it. Over the years we had put pieces together, especially since she'd come home for palliative care, but now we knew time was running out. I didn't want it to be a last-minute thing, and I didn't think we would be in much of a state to think about it once it happened anyway. Besides, we wanted Shelbs and the other children to have a say in it. So, the children gave ideas about what to do at the church, suggesting, for example, having bubbles for the children to blow as Shelbs loved bubbles, and having pink and red balloons, because these were her favourite colours, and everyone wearing pink and red. We chose songs with Shelbie, so she got a say in what songs we'd have. We took her to the crematorium so she knew where we would say our goodbyes. We asked her if she wanted a special bench or something similar at Whitemead to remember her by. We also asked her if we could scatter some of her ashes in the little stream there, so a part of her would always be a part of Whitemead. The church we attend has a sister church which is a lot bigger than ours. Knowing that there would be a lot of people coming on the day, we decided the service should be there, so we took Shelbs one Sunday so she knew where her celebration of life would take place. She would smile if she liked an idea, or turn away and sigh if she didn't, so she (along with her siblings) was a part of every decision. One Sunday afternoon when it was just me and Shelbs at home, I wrote letters to her daddy, brothers and sisters, nieces and some of her close friends to have after she'd gone. I tried writing each letter thinking of how she saw that particular person, as if they were her words. Then I read them out to her and asked if they were OK and she smiled. We drew around her hand, coloured it in and I helped her sign her name on each one.

In March, we had Shelbie's annual review at school and we announced at the meeting that we had visited an opportunities centre, as Shelbs was due to leave school in the July. We had visited the centre and it had a music room, a sensory room and hydro pool, all her favourite things. The staff there were lovely, and Shelbie had enjoyed her visit. So that was the plan. We told them we would always be back to visit once she left. School was happy for her and asked about her going to the prom. She had been two years before when she had gone up to post-sixteen. I approached her school teacher about her going back full-time for the last few months of school as she had been so well. She agreed that Shelbie would most certainly be able to cope, so we decided that she would start back after the Easter holidays on a full-time basis.

Our Children

This is a poem I wrote for all my children quite a few years ago. I had a lot of miscarriages after that one I had mentioned when my dad died, four of them when I was quite far gone and after having four in a row and nearly dying from haemorrhaging twice, it brought me back to this poem and reminded me how lucky I was with what I had: seven beautiful children

Looking out of the window there's trees blowing in the wind
Flowers blossoming, children laughing, how wonderful this world is.
Yet we abuse all this, we take for granted what could so easily be taken from us.

Do we appreciate what we're living for? No, we just want more
Do we thank God for the roof over our head? No, we just want a bigger house
Do we always smile when we think of our children? No, we just moan they're not good.

But today, maybe we should stop a while, just see the silence as peace and remember why we are here.
We're here to love and show our children love,
We're here to grow and give our children a future.

These little faces are faces of innocence, ones we should protect, a life to be thankful for.
We should look at our future, the children are what make it all happen,
Makes life the beauty it is today.

Chapter Eleven

Nick and I had been having discussions about planning for the future and working this into life with Shelbie as things stood. The kids had been asking for a puppy, and we'd so far refused, thinking it was something for after Shelbs had been promoted. But after months of talking about it we decided to go for it — Shelbs could end up being here with us for years, who knows, and our lives had to go on, and sometimes you just have to bite the bullet and go for it. So, we decided we would get a dog. Kalan's birthday was coming up and he wanted a German shepherd so much we thought that he could have one for his birthday. We were due to pick a puppy up at the end of the week, although Shelbie hadn't had the best few days — nothing in particular, but she certainly wasn't one hundred per cent. We'd had quite a few tears throughout the week, but she was well enough to be in school. She went in on the Friday which was her favourite day because it was choir day. Shelbie was in the choir, she used to lead the music, and only a few weeks had passed since we'd been to her choir concert. Nick was going but I had to work, but thankfully the class teacher said we would walk to the secondary site with our class and watch it. I was so grateful for that. It was funny watching her because, as she took the lead, the other children had to wait for her to play before they could start, and her hand would hover over the control and she'd smile, knowing everyone was waiting for her to commence proceedings. That was her cheeky personality all over. She only did a half day on this particular Friday as Nick had to drive a long way to collect the pup. She was OK with the nurse in the afternoon, and while the nurse was getting her bedtime stuff ready for me, I brought her into the lounge for her tea. We generally sit together for meals as a family, but Friday is always a do-what-you-like-and-pick-your-own-tea day, so we sat in the lounge to have tea while watching the TV. We had started the blended diet with Shelbs, and although it took a few years to get there completely, she was now off her liquid feed and just having blended food and was doing very well indeed. I still couldn't believe that her stomach had started working again after eight years. Just goes to show that it's never too late to try something.

I pushed some food into Shelbie, via the syringe — this was done slowly otherwise she would vomit, and it would generally take about an hour to feed her — so after I pushed some in, I knew I had time to shoot to the toilet for a wee. I was only gone minutes, but when I came back in the room Shelbie was cyanosed. I grabbed her O_2 and bagged her and she was OK. This wasn't unusual for her, she did this weekly, if not more often, so I finished giving her her tea then got her ready for bed.

About an hour or so later she did it again after she had gone onto her ventilator. This was a bit of a mystery to us and the respiratory team too: how can you stop breathing when a machine is doing it for you? I expect by now though you're not overly surprised, considering it's Shelbie. Her sats went down to fifteen and it took a while to get her breathing again, but I did. It's not unheard of for Shelbs to stop breathing twice in one day, but it is less common. After this second episode Shelbie was very unsettled and tearful, and again this was unusual. She finally settled about eleven o'clock that night.

Nick arrived home about half an hour later with the new pup (which Kalan named Lola). Whenever Nick went out, the first thing he'd ask is how Shelbs had been. I explained what had happened and said something wasn't right, and that we'd have to keep an eye because she was not a happy bunny. The following day she still wasn't quite herself but seemed a bit perkier. We had an OK morning, but then after lunch we had tears again all afternoon. We tried different analgesics and sedatives, we increased the sedatives she was on, we were doing anything to make her comfortable, but nothing seemed to work. She would just fall asleep for short bursts from sheer exhaustion. We put her to bed early in the end, and gave her her sleeping drugs, to try to give her some relief.

Shelbie had an unsettled night and was the same on Sunday, crying continually. We put her on regular two-hourly morphine and eventually this seemed to be working in her system along with clobazam. We kept the sofa bed out that we used at night in the lounge and laid on it with her. Our pastor, Andrew, had popped around for something and he prayed over Shelbie, that she would be at peace and not in pain. Just as he finished praying, Shelbie decided to stop breathing. Andrew said, 'I know I asked for peace for her, but I didn't mean that much peace, I didn't mean for you to take her, Lord.' We all had a chuckle at this, she started breathing again, and all was good. Ish.

Shelbs was on strong drugs just to keep her settled but it took until Monday for her to be a bit more comfortable, as even changing her pad was upsetting her. She just seemed to be in so much pain. We called the GP out and he said that, other than a few crackles on her chest, there was nothing obvious. He started her on oral antibiotics just to err on the side of caution.

He returned the following day, but Shelbs was no better and was now not emptying her bowels. She hadn't had her stoma bag emptied since the previous day and, as we could empty that bag six times a day normally, it was very unusual for there to be nothing in it. She also had a very high temperature and the doctor warned us this could be it. 'This is the worst I've seen her,' were his actual words. The district nurses were informed and they contacted Little Bridge House as it was decided we would go back down the following morning for end of life. They wanted us to go that day but I needed to get my head around it all. I knew that this was it. I could feel it. Well, maybe not so much feel it, but certainly I didn't feel any hope as I had done before. Even when things were bad, I still gripped in my gut the chance of hope. But not this time.

I rang just a handful of people to let them know — Mike, Gareth and Zoë, Margarita and Jane, and Annmarie, all of whom had seen her regularly and kept up the contact and support for us since she'd been that ill in September. In the evening, Gareth and Zoë and Margarita and Jane came over to support us. We ended up going through photos to put together for a slide show that my nephew, Joe, was doing for us for Shelbie's funeral. I felt sick that we going there again seven months after the first 'end of life' visit. I should have been packing really, but instead I chose to sit and do the photos. Once everyone had left we went around and gave Dave and Christel the news. (They're an elderly couple we know and love, whom we'd met at our old church. They became good friends, but more like family to us. They'd been like grandparents to all the kids but particularly to Shelbs: they adored her and she loved them dearly.)

We kept Shelbie's night nurse, because it was her favourite one and I kind of knew it would be the last chance she would have with her, but we slept downstairs anyway as we didn't want to be far away from her. We didn't sleep well. I could see Shelbie's bedroom light keep going on and I could hear a bit of commotion in there, and I wanted to go in but knew that the nurse would get me straight away if I were needed. I was told in the morning that she had been vomiting all night. We told Courtney what was happening but, as the older boys were both working, we felt it best to wait and see what Little Bridge House said before we rushed everyone down as we had before. The GP, district nurses and palliative nurse all came round that morning. Dave and Christel also popped in to see her, all just to say their goodbyes.

The nurses gave Shelbie an anti-sickness drug so she would have a settled journey on the way down but she reacted really badly to it. She was being violently sick continuously for over three hours (bizarrely, the amount of time the drug was supposed to keep her settled for the journey, so I guess she was sick until it was in her system no longer). I hadn't seen her be that sick even with a stomach bug, and this delayed our leaving for Little Bridge House. We felt she was just getting worse and worse, and that if we didn't leave fairly soon it would be too late to go anywhere.

I put off packing for as long as I could, because I just knew it would be the last time I would be doing this. Also, of course, we needed to pack all the extras we needed if Shelbie died — the same as we did last time, but it seemed even harder now. Once we were packed, I knew we had to head off with her for potentially the last time. Once we returned it could — probably would — be without her. She might never see or sleep in her bedroom again. This was unbearable.

Once the vomiting settled, we left. We needed to get her there and settled, and thankfully the journey was pretty stable. On arrival the staff at Little Bridge House just let her be for the day as she wasn't too distressed. She had an OK night as long as she was left alone. Dr Bruce saw Shelbie and said he had seen her worse, and he agreed with the GP that although there were a few crackles on her chest, there was nothing he was concerned about. And he expected that if there was any infection the antibiotics should have started kicking in. He wasn't happy that she hadn't had her bowels open since Monday, though, three days ago now.

We had stopped feeding her the day before to give her complete gut rest and he agreed this was best. But she wouldn't stay like that, he added. She would either start pooing again, which would be fab because she may just start improving, or her gut would start leaking to other areas of her body and she would just get worse. It could go one way or the other.

At this point in time, her body was starting to shut down. We hadn't started the syringe driver at home, so Dr Bruce got her started on one to make her more comfortable. He checked on her a little later in the day. No change. We had brought Courtney and Aria down with us but needed now to contact Rhys and Connor. We felt that they needed to be here as there were no improvements. We also let family and some friends know where we were at. It's funny, a few people said, 'Oh, you've been down this road before loads of times'. I think they said it to try to help, but it doesn't. You worry absolutely no less, and you don't need it almost dismissed, if you like, just because she'd been really ill before. Besides, she'd never come down for end-of-life care before September. Yes, she had been very ill but we had never gone to the hospice for potentially end of life. It was scary for us and something you certainly shouldn't have to go through more than once. These were my most difficult and darkest days.

Margarita and Jane brought the boys to the hospice for us, and while they were on their way, Shelbie did a poo. Not a little bit, she completely filled her stoma bag up. This was really good news, but so embarrassing when they all arrived and we had to explain that we'd had a breakthrough — it could just be constipation after all! Dr Bruce came back in to see Shelbs that evening and said, 'She's not shutting down any more. This is a real positive'. When Margarita, Jane and the boys turned up not long after, they were very understanding. We laughed about it and I'm sure they would have wanted to see Madam anyway.

The following day was a Friday and was pretty uneventful. We even managed to give Shelbs a bed bath and hair wash and she was a bit chatty, but then she started getting upset again. She was still on the syringe driver to keep her settled so we just left her alone as much as we could. Nick and I hadn't slept well all week, but Friday night we both were really unsettled. In the early hours of Saturday morning the nurse came to our room and asked if we were happy to have the driver increased as Shelbie was getting really upset, even just to have her pad changed or be turned. We agreed. We just wanted her out of pain.

Dr Bruce came to see Shelbs in the afternoon. He was happy with how she was progressing. We made plans to start feeding her again the following day. He suggested we start with something light and Nick said he would go to the shop and get baby rice in a bit. Woah! This is one conversation I hadn't expected. Before Dr Bruce left her room he said, 'I'm really happy, I think your young lady could just turn this around again. But then Shelbie always does the opposite of what I say.' Those were his exact words. He knew her only too well. He also said to leave the driver as it was for now, but to look at decreasing it when they'd found some other drugs to help her with her pain and discomfort. What she was normally on might not be enough, and the most important thing was to make her comfortable.

Things were again looking up, then. At this point I would normally take that breath I'd been holding and feel the relief that we would normally feel when she turned a corner, but I couldn't. It wasn't that I didn't believe the doctor. It was just something stopping me from believing that she would be OK.

Just after Dr Bruce had seen her, Mike, Esther and their kids came into see Shelbs. We sat with her, chatting for a while, and, as she had been very unsettled, I laid in bed with her and sang 'Father's Eyes' and 'Amazing Grace'. Shelbie hadn't been settled all morning, but as I sang, she cwtched straight into me and settled, and after a while I put her Mr Tumble teddy in my place, so she was cuddling into him. Mike and Esther were with Shelbs most of the afternoon, while their children were in and out playing with our kids, which was probably quite good for my lot. Shelbie had a moment where she seemed to need suctioning but we weren't clearing anything. I noticed the noise was different to normal and remembered hearing it when I was with other people when they died. A nurse took me to another room and explained what it was, and I got a bit funny with her. I knew what was happening and I didn't need it explaining, and Nick couldn't cope with being told anything at that moment anyway. On reflection I totally appreciate what she was doing, she wasn't in the wrong, I just couldn't take what I already knew being said out loud. I said to Esther that I needed some air so we went to the back garden attached to the room we were staying in. While we were chatting, I explained to Esther that despite how things were looking I didn't feel that Shelbs was going to pull through this time, despite the positive signs we had been given just hours before. I said that I had spoken to Shelbs earlier in the day and told her God was waiting for her and it was OK for her to go. She didn't need to stay for us. As much as we would miss her, we didn't want her in pain. I said to her, 'If you're in pain and uncomfortable you need to go where there will be no more pain, no limits, total freedom. A place to walk and talk.' Nick had told her weeks before that she had his blessing to go, it was so hard for him to say, but he did because he loved her so much.

After a while, Nick and Mike joined us outside. Nick said Shelbs was still settled and stable. She was on less than half a litre of O_2 with sats in the high nineties, and she wasn't on the ventilator (as this seemed to make her more distressed than actually help), so she was managing all by herself. Her breathing had been amazing all week, considering. There were times when she needed the ventilator but when we had been at home, we hadn't been able to get her off it — it was needed all the time for days. But these last few days she was worse on it, even at night.

After ten minutes or so, Nick said he was just nipping to the toilet, and we all carried on chatting. After a little while I said to Esther and Mike, 'Nick's been a while' — not realising at this point that he'd already had to go back to Shelbie's room — so we decided to go back in. I nipped to the loo in our room on the way back. I was in the bathroom and noticed Shelbie's sats monitor had been going off for quite a while and as I came out of the bathroom the nurses were standing by my door. They told me that Shelbs' sats were low — sixty — despite giving her ten litres of O_2. I knew this was it. I ran into her room and realised then I needed to call Rhys, Connor and Kalan back. They were at the cinema, and Mac, Cienna, Sophia, Courtney and Aria had gone out with the sibling workers. I'd been glad of that because they hadn't wanted to leave Shelbs, especially Mac and Cie, but they needed that break, that moment of fun. The others were all back now but the three boys weren't.

I rang Rhys. 'Where are you?' He said that they were literally stepping onto the bus and were thinking of going to the pub. I told him they needed to get back right now as Shelbs wasn't good. I didn't want to tell them on the phone she was dying, but I needed them to know the urgency of the situation. The bus ride was only ten minutes, but Mike drove down to meet them off the bus.

I went back in to Shelbs and prayed for her to hold on until they got back. I could see the huge change in her breathing. The boys came back and we made sure Courtney and the others were in the room too. I explained to all my children that this was Shelbie's time.

Mac said, 'She's not dying, is she?'

I had to tell him. 'Yes, I think this is it now.'

In a panicky voice he said, 'No, not right now.' He just kept saying it. I don't think he could quite believe this was actually going to happen. He was crying.

Kalan and Connor were laid over her sobbing, in fact Connor was holding her so tight I had to say, 'Son, I know she's dying anyway, but you're crushing her, she literally can't breathe.' A last laugh with the nurses.

About twenty minutes after we all sat with her, Shelbs took her last breath. We had played music to her constantly since we'd been there because we knew how much she loved it and I didn't ever want her left in silence. We had YouTube on, literally any song could have come on, but she took her final breaths to 'O Come To The Altar' and the words playing at the time were:

Are you hurting and broken within, o come to the altar, the Father's arms are open wide. Come today there's no reason to wait. Bring your sorrows and trade them for joy, from the ashes a new life is born. Bow down before him.

These words caught me. The exact words for her final breath were, O come to the altar, as if He was talking to her, calling her and she heard it and replied, 'OK, Lord, I'm on my way.' This song was no coincidence.

As Shelbie took her final breath, Mike and Esther's eldest, Mally, had come to join us, not knowing it would be at that exact time. He stood there and just said, 'Well, that's awkward...' Even in the worst times ever a child can still bring a light, a smile. It is something that still makes me chuckle now, even though I did feel for him at the time. Bless him, he was only fourteen.

A little while later, Shelbie was taken to Starborn, a beautiful temperature-controlled room where your child can stay for a week or so after they die so you can be with them as much as you like. It was actually opposite the bedroom we were staying in and there was no pressure on the children: they could go and see her if they wished, but it didn't matter if not. She didn't look comfortable and her arms weren't right. They were by her side, yet Shelbie always slept with her arms behind her head (well, since her stroke, just the one arm). I asked the nurse to move it, and she then agreed it looked more like Shelbie now.

When we went back in the following morning, her appearance had changed completely. It wasn't our imagination in grief. It had changed. She was smiling as if she was saying, 'It's OK, I'm OK.' When we told the nurses they just smiled. I think they thought we were seeing things until they went in and saw for themselves how 'happy' she looked. We were in and out to Shelbie the whole week. Someone asked if Aria and Sophia had managed to go into Shelbie without feeling uncomfortable and yes, they had. I went in once to find them both sat on the end of the bed eating crisps and chatting away, and that was fine. I didn't want them to feel it was anything bad, they had to feel comfortable with it all. Maybe not quite that comfortable, but it didn't matter. I hope that they realise that death isn't something you need to be scared of. Just before we went home Shelbie was taken to the chapel of rest at the funeral directors. Aria and Sophia kissed her goodbye and didn't bat an eyelid, they didn't say she was cold or that they didn't want to kiss her, they did it so naturally and I'm glad. That's how we want them to look at death — as something natural, and not to fear.

It was Easter Sunday the day after she had been picked up and the day we were going home. Our last Easter with Shelbie, and our first without her.

None of what happened over those coming weeks was coincidental. It all had purpose. At her "celebration of life" (it was a celebration because despite nineteen years not being long enough, it was nineteen years more than Charlie had, and also a lot longer than we thought we would have with her) we tried to make everything have meaning to

Shelbs. She had already picked what was happening for her day, whenever her day would be. She even picked the bench she wanted at Whitemead, and we took her to the shop to pick it. We had the red and pink balloons, the red and pink dress code, we had rainbow roses — because they are bright and quirky — tied together by the tape that used to hold her airway in. She loved balloons. And all the children were given the bubbles as we had planned. We had twelve songs because music was Shelbie's love. If you wanted her to be vocal and lively, this was best achieved by putting music on and getting the instruments out, and if the little ones joined in it would hype her up even more. These were her favourite times. Her coffin was rainbow wicker — something different and very fitting to Shelbie, and when Sophia talks about it, she always calls it her special rainbow bed.

The day was perfect and exactly how Shelbs would have wanted and chosen it.

A lot was said about the type of person she was. Some of the things said to describe her passed comment on her smile. In fact, everyone who'd met her over the years would comment on her smile and how she would smile with her eyes. They said when you met Shelbie there was something about her, she just brought you into her life. She would speak to you, really speak to you, although not by mouth. People would say they had never met someone so vulnerable yet so strong. She had an amazing gift for connection, and for human interaction in a way that has been lost in our society. Margarita said that Shelbie revolutionised the school curriculum in the way that she was. So, she taught them how to teach children like herself. She had no words but her communication was more powerful than the most articulate person in the whole world. Someone said that even though she was limited in her body, she didn't allow it to define her.

Pastor John Hall, our old pastor from the church we had attended before, spoke about Shelbie. He said that when he baptised her five years ago, he remembered understanding Shelbie more and her faith, and who she was as a woman, and who she was as a woman of God. A particular scripture really touched him — that it's not what we look like on the outside but it's what is in the heart that matters. What he learnt from Shelbie was, as he put it, 'Her body was knackered in so many different ways, it was bust up, it wasn't working well, but what was key to this girl, it was her heart. What you can learn, and I've learnt over the years, is that this girl had a heart. In the Bible it describes a guy called David as a man after God's own heart. And I believe that Shelbie was a woman after God's own heart. But she gave her heart, she gave all that she had and she gave all that she was to God, and to her family, and to those that knew her and those that loved her. A verse from the Bible typifies the woman of God that we remember. I have fought the good fight, (and we saw that fight in her). This is Shelbie. I have finished the race, I have kept the faith, now there is in store for me — *for Shelbie now there is in store for her* — the crown of righteousness, which the Lord, the righteous judge will award me on that day.'

There are no better ways to describe her, and I will take with me forever that comfort that she "fought the good fight" and has been rewarded because of it. She deserved more than ever to be rewarded and to have peace, rest and be free of pain in a place where there is only beauty after the work she did here on earth. A lot of people believe that once you die there is nothing, it's all over. I couldn't disagree more. Shelbie not only got into Heaven with the King of Kings. She has gone to work for God, and she may be an angel right now watching down on each of her siblings and nieces guiding them.

We didn't have flowers from other people and we didn't have them for her name. Instead, Mike made us wooden letters spelling "Shelbie" and all of our children and grandchildren decorated them. It was beautiful. Connor decided he wanted to write messages on one of the letters instead. His words were lovely. He wrote:

Have fun with our brother, don't kick him in the head too much. Love your wheelchair, race driver. Don't worry, I'll pull Mummy's hair out for you and I'll kick some people in the leg so they don't forget your big whacker boots. Fly high my little warrior.

Mac also wrote on his.

To Shelbie, I love you, I always have and my life has changed loads without you. You're in peace. I have always loved you and will continue to do so from Mac.

Rhys and Connor carried her "special rainbow bed" into the church along with Tyler, one of her taxi drivers she loved and Craig, one of her favourite school teachers. The taxi company who used to take Shelbs to school drove us to the church and back with some of her old drivers. They didn't charge a penny, and they helped make it so special by the way they were with us all. Whitemead, where we always camped, put on the celebration after the service in the venue and some of the staff came to her funeral. The music was played perfectly by Gareth and the team at our church. In fact, our church made it all look so beautiful and run so smoothly.

I often picture that day. There isn't much I can remember about it, but on some days, I can't believe just how well it went. It was exactly the vision we had tried to give Shelbie of it. But on other days it is so painful. I just cannot believe it's done now. It's over. While we had prepared for that day, we hoped that we would never see it, or at least not yet, but at the same time I knew it was coming and it hurts so, so much. Because Shelbie's camping place at Whitemead was so important to her, at some point we will scatter some of her ashes in the stream in the woods where we used to walk with her, as we told her we would. And on her twentieth birthday we plan to put a bench near the swimming pool where she spent so many happy times, so we can sit and remember her. Not that we need a bench, of course, as she is on our minds twenty-four-seven anyway, but it is still going to be a special place because it was so special to our little princess.

We have a teddy that Shelbs had made years before which had always sat on her bed. We told her we would put some of her ashes inside it so that a part of her would always still be at home and we will carry that through. It was something else she was part of making the decision about. Some people have said it's a bit creepy and would make them feel uncomfortable, if that's the case I'm definitely doing it because that would make Shelbie laugh.

I close my eyes sometimes and try to imagine her smell. I can still remember it for now, but it does worry me that one day I will try to think of the smell and it just won't come. I can remember kissing her neck and I would always sniff her. She had the best smell — she had a slight baby smell to her — and, besides, she really loved it when I sniffed her. It would always make her chuckle. I heard on the TV recently someone say of fear, 'Don't be afraid to be afraid. Use it. Use your fear to think of how you can help someone who is more frightened than you.' It made me wonder if that's how Shelbie would feel sometimes. Did she feel frightened at times, but turned it to wondering how we were feeling and so helped us through instead of worrying about how she had been feeling? She did understand a lot more than she had speech and I always felt that how we were as a family was more important to her than what she felt. She was selfless and, even on the days you could see she wasn't in the mood, she would still sit there and give us the most beautiful smile. I could see her eyes and what they were saying, and maybe she didn't realise that, but she always tried giving us her best and succeeded, even when I told her it was OK to have off days.

Our home has never been the same. Someone said when she went, 'Shelbie is the heartbeat of your family.' How do you carry on without a heartbeat? We've had to, of course, but since walking through those doors after getting back from Little Bridge House, it has never been the same and can never be the same. We still have a lot of love there to give, but there is always that void.

Someone else said to me a while ago, 'When you lose a child, you're stood in a room but it's like you're behind a glass, you're there in the room with everyone else, but not quite there, you'll never be completely there again.' That is the best description ever. Spot on.

When we used to go out or go away it was like a military operation, especially when visiting Little Bridge House. Coming home was the worst, we would get the kids out and have to unload the car straight away and get all of Shelbie's equipment out as we would need it all, so it was never an option to think, 'Ah, let's have a cuppa first then unpack.' It had to be done immediately. Now we seem to have all the time in the world. We're still late for everything, mind, but that's just me! Shelbs just never used to help by pulling her bag off just as we were about to leave for somewhere or vomiting or not breathing, but in terms of punctuality, nothing has changed there.

That first time, walking back into the house, was torture and we knew then our home would never be the same again. It was so different from when we had been there two weeks before that. We did, though, still have that puppy to contend with, although she had met Shelbie which I don't think was a coincidence. I feel like when we got Lola, Shelbs thought, 'Right, now is my time. I can go. My brothers and sisters have someone else to focus on.' And Lola was a good distraction. The kids fell in love with her and she didn't understand we were grieving. As a puppy she still had demands that needed to be met and the children threw everything into her. Less than three months after Shelbie died, Lola got ill at just five months old and we found out she had a rare kidney disease that was causing kidney failure. She died less than two weeks after we were told about it, despite trying every treatment there was available. "Just a dog" some might say, but so much more to my children. It broke Kalan when we had to have Lola put down. I just couldn't take any more, I just couldn't believe that these precious kids had to go through another death for someone they loved so much. Lola was obviously nowhere near close to what Shelbs meant to them but she had been such good therapy. It was unbearable. Our house had lost that atmosphere once Shelbs went, it was eerily quiet waiting for the sound of her playing with her bells and just lacking that presence you could feel, but the kids had had a focus. And now that was gone too.

We got another pup in the hope that they could refocus, another German shepherd called Gracie. She is fantastic, but the children have found it hard to fall for her completely, maybe getting to a point of trying to protect themselves, I guess. Perhaps it wasn't the right decision, but none of us know what is right or how someone will react. We just have to go on what we feel at the time and actually, maybe I needed her as much as the children did.

When Shelbie was first promoted, I think I lived in denial. Every time I thought about it, it hurt, so I stopped thinking, pushed it aside, trying to persuade myself it was OK during the day, as Shelbs was at school. And Nick struggled first thing as he did her morning routine. He would get her up and bring her into the conservatory. I would come down to find her having her breakfast. We would discuss what kind of night she'd had, and what her blood sugars had been before breakfast, what was planned for her day, that kind of thing. Then I would tell her how clever she was or how naughty she was depending on what she had been up to. She would just smile, because she didn't actually care, all that stuff was for the rest of us to worry about.

Chapter Twelve

The worst part of the day for me is around teatime. Shelbie would sit at the table with us and have her tea. That space is always empty now. Then I would do her "evening cares". Once settled, she would have a story and often watch TV with one of the kids. The children had a chores chart, the older ones all had one when they were younger, including Shelbie. She would have to help Mummy hoover (she usually just ended up whacking me and the dog with the hoover end) and she had to help Mummy make her bed. Oh, my word, that was hard work because every time I went to move her away from the bedding she would grab the duvet, which then made the bed "unmade" again. And she also had to help mummy dust the TV unit, although what she actually did was keep turning the volume up, so that the music was blaring. But she had her chores on a list all the same. We felt it important, firstly that she felt included, but also so the older ones didn't feel they were having to do stuff and not Shelbs. If she could do it, then we would make her as an example to them. So, the younger ones now had charts, on their charts would be, "Read Shelbie a bedtime story" or, "Give Shelbie her nebuliser". They keep asking me when I'm going to redo the chart but I can't. I just cannot bring myself to take it down and change it. Not yet.

Now, once teatime is over, we clear up together in about five minutes and don't know what to do with our time. I hate sitting in the seat next to where Shelbie would be sat for tea. It just reminds you how many places she is missing from.

Five weeks after Shelbie got her promotion to Heaven, Courtney gave birth to a little girl, Nellie. A new life is a miracle, I always say that, but it was bittersweet. I was in the hospital for the few days Courtney was in and I felt as though I couldn't breathe sometimes. Everything about the place reminded me of Shelbie. Usually in a hospital I would feel right at home, because it was my life for so long. I always felt as though I belonged, and I never felt intimidated or uncomfortable. But now I was feeling a bit of fear — every tape or monitor would remind me of what I had lost only five weeks before, but at the same time this was about Courtney and what she was going through. She gave us a new life in our family, and a new focus. It is so sad Shelbie never got to meet Nellie, never got to hold her and give her the famous slap on top of her head as she did with every other baby she came into contact with. But Nellie has become another welcomed distraction. She is so like Shelbie as well, there's definitely a part of her in Nellie, maybe she has met her in a way we don't understand!

A few months on and we felt we were falling apart at times, feeling so lost, empty, angry that life hurts so much. The pain, the twisting sick feeling in my stomach — some days it felt unbearable. I would talk to God. I'm not angry with Him. How can I be when He blessed me in the beginning with this precious, unique, little soul? But every time I tried to talk to Him something was in the way. It was like there was a brick wall. The best I could do was listen to worship music, keep hearing those words and believing them, and hoping for a day when the pain is more bearable. I guess, if I'm honest, I'm a bit jealous. He now gets to spend those enjoyable, mischievous, fun filled days with her.

I know though this isn't going to be our life forever. He isn't done with us yet, but I just can't physically imagine moving on and having a new kind of life. In between all the hard work we got to smell her, kiss her, hold her in our arms... We have so many memories, but memories don't let you do these things any more, memories don't fill those empty arms, memories don't move on with you. We can't make any new memories that will include her, and that's hard to imagine.

Another thing I can't bear is meeting new people and them not knowing Shelbie as part of us. We will never be able to show her off again. I loved that. I was so proud of her. I used to love how people would spend just a short time with her before realising there was so much more to her than meets the eye. It's hard to accept how quickly things change. How Shelbie is already being left out of things by others. People assume that by not mentioning her or leaving her memory out of something they're saving us pain, but they don't realise they are, in fact, making things worse. I want her name spoken daily, I want to scream it out to keep her out there. The people who think they are helping just need to maybe learn to ask, rather than to assume. I didn't realise how quickly people would pull away and we would feel so alone. Some people said they kept back to give us time to grieve, but we need so much to be busy, to have people around us. We already have too much time, approximately twenty-four hours a day, in fact, that has been left empty from Shelbie leaving.

We felt we needed carrying, but that is a big thing to ask of people who have their own lives and families. Everyone is already so busy. This isn't a criticism, just an honest reflection of how we felt — still feel, in fact. It is a lonely place to be.

We do have a handful of people that have always been supportive and it wouldn't feel right not to mention them because they helped carry us, but then it always seemed to fall on that same few. We couldn't keep asking again and so we carry on struggling on our own, but maybe we shouldn't because their arms are open for us.

When someone is in need, we often wait for them to ask for help, but being the person who has often had to ask for that help, I know it is horrible to keep asking. Maybe there is a lesson there for us all. If you know someone is struggling, don't wait for them to ask for help. Often, they won't, or certainly not until it's too late. No one wants to be a burden and ask for help, and it's so much easier to accept help if it's specifically offered. "If I can do anything…" is often genuine but it was so much more supportive when Shelbs was in and out of hospital and a few people asked, 'What can I do? What needs doing?'

It just felt like someone was holding their arms out and saying, 'Let me carry you, let me take the little bits that I can on my back to lighten your load.'

We want Shelbie's name kept alive, in fact we need her name kept alive, for us and also for other people because they are still going to keep learning about her and from her. We will make sure of that.

When Shelbie first died it was too painful at first to even think about, let alone write down how I was feeling, and how we were feeling as a family. Mac struggles with the fact that's she's actually gone. What thirteen-year-old can actually comprehend "forever"? He felt that because she had done it in the past, this time also she would still "turn it around". We had many discussions while we were at Little Bridge House about whether she would go this time. Mac said he didn't want her to go. I had to explain that none of us wanted her to go but now she was always in pain and the bad times were starting to outweigh the good, and that wasn't fair on her. It's not fair on the family that love her to be without her, but it was more unfair for her to be suffering because that wasn't living, that was just existing, and Shelbie's whole being was about living. She was here to enjoy life and, if she couldn't enjoy it, she had to go.

Mac asked me many times if I thought this time was it and I did, I truly did, but I didn't want to tell him for definite because if she had gone a bit longer, he would have been less and less prepared. He would always assume that she would "turn it around". You become complacent. So, I told him, 'Yes, I think it probably is her time now, I'm pretty sure it is, but no one knows except her and God.'

We can protect our kids from many things, but not this, not death, and not the pain that comes after. But never, not even when I watch them suffering, do I have regrets because months of pain and forever missing her were made up for by her very existence. What she gave when she was here. Life is for learning, not regretting. It will take a long time for them to see that, but they will. She will have taught them things they won't even realise right now. One day they will be grateful for having had the chance to know and love her, to be blessed to have an extra special child in their lives, in their family.

Chapter Thirteen

We cook our first roast dinner a few months after Shelbie's promotion. Nothing special, true, but the first one since she'd gone. I hadn't even thought about it when I invited the older kids around, but as I'm preparing the vegetables it suddenly hits me: this is the first roast without Shelbs, the one time when we would all come together and sit for a meal. I look in the freezer for the peas, and there's her kale and butternut squash. No one else would eat this but I always made sure I had it in case we're having a meal that wasn't good for her tummy, like a curry, that she wouldn't like.

Shelbie won't be sat in her place. As I'm putting the veg in the pan, I go to put extra in for her to make up some meals for the week. I always do too much and then blend and freeze it for her. I still have the veg in the freezer, as well as her frozen fruit. Thinking about it, her last meal is still in the fridge, missing the half she'd had. I just can't get rid of any of it. I realise that I don't need as much veg, so I take some peas back out and feel sick. Every time I open the freezer it hits me that there's no frozen meals made up for her in there. What's worse is that sometimes I forget what those spaces are for. Were for. I almost feel guilty that I've put something else in that space.

I so desperately want her back in that moment. Life isn't completely empty, it can't be with a new life in our family, but it is so suffocating at times. You feel you can't catch your breath. The house just suddenly felt emptier. It reminds you that even though she wasn't as vocal towards the end, her presence just spoke volumes. Perhaps we hadn't realised just how much.

While I'm cooking tea, to keep her entertained and distracted (as she would be getting tired and hungry by this point), right now she would be playing with her bells or I would have her in the kitchen and she would have my phone to listen to music and I would sing along to her. Or she would watch *Mr Tumble* and that would be blaring from her TV. I ask,

'Oh Shelbie, how do we ever move forwards? How do we ever accept you won't be here again? We can't kiss you, can't hug you. We love you so, so much.' I never knew my heart could break even more since Charlie and Grampy left, but this pain is so unbearable. I don't know how I'm still going. We were literally putting one foot in front of the other some days — most days — and I can't see that changing.

There are days we laugh, but the laughter sometimes feels a bit fake. Well, that said, I deliberately watch things on TV that I know will make me laugh, but it's like I have to keep laughing to ensure I can't cry. Maybe we just need to do it until it feels real and until I am ready to separate the two. Tears and laughter, laughter and tears. It's real when we're remembering Shelbs though. She always made us chuckle, even now.

I was watching Sophia dancing to music in the lounge, her and Aria often do this, and Shelbs would sit on the sofa next to me, or in her chair, watching them and either smile or look at me in disbelief. I would sometimes put Shelbs on the floor, but that wouldn't put them off, they would dance round her or even over her. It wasn't unusual for them to jump over her and she would often stick her arm out to trip them up, still smiling. We have a video of them playing a game where they'd run around her and she had to try to get them with her hand and trip them up. She was good at that game and usually won. That was when we were camping at Whitemead on Mother's Day, just two weeks before she died.

There was something else I did. I moved the furniture around in the lounge but made sure that I left enough space everywhere for her wheelchair. It's funny what you do without even thinking about it.

The next horrible event was Father's Day. I was dreading it for Nick. It was so painful for him. He coped better than I thought he would, but there were quite a few tears. On the way into church, Sophia turned to me and said, 'Don't cry when we go in here today, all right? I don't want to hear that noise, it makes me sad.'

After church we went to the woodland where my dad's ashes are to put down a gift. As we got there the heavens opened, so I decided to go on my own while Nick and the kids waited in the car. I couldn't find my umbrella so had to use Sophia's princess one. I imagined how much Shelbs would be laughing at me. I walked to where my dad was and told him, 'How the tables have turned. It was always a daughter desperately missing her dad, and now sat in the car is a dad desperately missing his daughter.'

I got back to the car — it was still raining — and Sophia said, 'Shelbie, you're so naughty. She must have pressed the rain button.' At her funeral it had tipped down too, but I knew it would be because she loved water so much.

As we'd come out of the church, Craig, her teacher, had said, 'One more water play, Shelbs.'

A few days before Father's Day, Sophia had been on Shelbie's swing. She turned to me and said, 'Oh, I miss Shelbie, and you do, Nainy... but Jesus fixed her legs and she can walk and talk. How cool's that?' She has brought so much laughter for us. I love how kids talk so freely, and how Sophia says things straight out, not being worried about whether she upsets us or if it's awkward or whatever. She just comes straight out with it. It's so refreshing and always puts me in a better place with her beautiful comments.

Aria, maybe being a bit younger, hasn't said so much, although she did look to Shelbie's bedroom door a few weeks after Shelbs had gone and said, 'Shelbie, come back now,' as if she was saying, OK, it's been long enough.

I said, 'No, darling, we'd love her to come back but she can't, can she? She has to stay in Heaven.' That really got to my heart. It must be so confusing for a three-year-old.

There are just so many reminders, and so many things happen that make me think Shelbie is still having a say and is still around in a way. I was driving to her school for her Remembrance Day a few months back. It was a beautiful day with the children from her class sharing various memories, but it was also a very tearful time. I hadn't appreciated how much her death would affect them, especially her close friends, but they genuinely loved and missed her. I was on my way there after a night looking after my nan and running late (for a change!) but there was a road closed so I knew it would be busier. On planning my trip, I knew that one particular way wasn't an easy route. I found the other way easier, but as it would be busier due to the road closure, I needed to take the more difficult route really. But I chose the easier way. When I got onto the road it was at a standstill. I knew I would miss the start of the assembly. While sat in the traffic something spoke to me and all I could hear was, 'Sometimes the easier route to take isn't always the right route to take, that's why we need to step out in faith and sometimes do what we're not comfortable doing.' At the first opportunity I turned off that road to get on to the other route and do you know what? That road was actually clear, and I made Shelbie's assembly.

There is a definite lesson in there and it made me realise that, although it's tough right now and we want to hide away, taking the easy option and not dealing with what's really going on isn't the answer. When we step out of our comfort zone, and take the route we know is tougher, but could have a better outcome, at the end we will see the benefit all the more. It really spoke to me and I felt I'd made a big step compared to the shuffling I had been doing. I even found that I could say Shelbie's name without crying every time. I guess that's nothing really, to read it on the page, but for me it was massive. And I was finding I could talk to God a bit more without feeling as if there was something in the way and, the more I talk to Him, the closer I feel to Shelbie. It's another step forwards for me, and it all started with one little change of route that day.

I woke up a few mornings later and spoke to God straight away with ease. The wall between us that Satan was trying to build was breaking down. In the midst of my grief, he saw my weakness and tried to weave his way in, but he can get stuffed! He has no place, no authority, but a lot to answer for in this world.

I find it funny how people often won't acknowledge God in the good times but as soon as something goes wrong, we call on Him immediately — often through desperation, but a lot of the time in anger, even if we supposedly don't believe in Him. It often makes me question whether people do subconsciously believe. People say they don't believe in ghosts, but when things are bad, they don't call out to a ghost, do they? People use the phrase "oh my God", but why use the name of someone you don't think exists? It just often makes me wonder.

This world gets so angry with God for bad things, yet we are always taught He is a God of love, He is about good not evil. Everyone knows the devil is evil, but he never gets the blame. We blame the person that made us, loves us, sees us as perfect in His eyes despite all our flaws. It's always baffled me how Satan, someone who still has a lot of power and who was once one of God's angels, doesn't instantly get the blame.

I've had the discussion with people that God allows these things to happen. Some bits I admit I don't understand so I am trusting that it will make sense when I get my promotion to Heaven. I do appreciate that some of it is God allowing free choice. The evils of this world don't make sense but I absolutely do not believe that a person who does save and performs miracles (and we witnessed enough of them ourselves with Madam) doesn't have a valid reason. That's not easy to hear when you are hurting and going through it, but when nothing else makes sense that's where faith steps in.

Shelbie had a lot of hurt and a lot of pain, yet she never stayed angry, she never blamed God, she just accepted that's how it was for her for whatever reason and that she still had a job to do: to teach as she did. That was far more important to her, so she did it every day with a smile and with an open heart.

Margarita, who had been our biggest support over the years and who's given that support wholeheartedly, said she'd never forget the time Shelbie was in the hospital in excruciating pain (this was before we knew she had the hole in her bowel). She had gone in to visit Shelbs and she said she was crying and blue from the pain. Margarita went home that night devastated at seeing her like that but went back the following day to find Shelbie rolling around clapping and smiling, despite the pain. It's a lesson for us all. I would have been moaning for weeks to anyone who would listen, and feeling genuinely very sorry for myself, not rolling around and smiling! Yet, that's exactly what Shelbie did. She just smiled and smiled and carried on. This went on for six months, being in this much pain, yet she smiled throughout. That is just a glimpse of how amazing my little girl was.

I was at my gran's one morning, after staying the night with her, and was saying a prayer, just asking God to help us through and saying how sorry I was that I hadn't chatted to Him much, but I had found it all so hard, when Shelbie seemed to appear. She looked exactly the same, except she now sat unaided, kind of crouching down. She looked at me, smiled and said, 'I can walk now.'

'I know you can,' I said, smiling back at her, and she ran off to play. That was it. Just that brief encounter. She had just popped into my prayer like a child who interrupts a conversation. That was what I noticed. Although she was nineteen, she spoke just like a child. Grief, maybe? Who knows, but it was a huge comfort that I needed at that time to keep going.

I was in church not long after this, taking communion as usual, and I couldn't hold the tears back. I had to go outside to catch my breath. I hadn't realised that it happened last time in church. I was fine until I had communion. I always used to break less than a crumb off and place it in Shelbie's mouth then I would rub the wine on her tongue. I always said to her, 'This is Jesus' flesh and this is His blood, this is to remind you He died for you because you are so special and He loves you. But you know that, don't you?' She would always smile as if in agreement. It was important that I reminded her and it was something significant between us. I just hadn't realised how important it was until now. We will get there, I know, but church feels so empty without her sitting there beside us.

A new guy came to church one week, and Nick and I were chatting to him at the end and all I could think was, 'You won't even know we had a child here, she should be sat in the middle of the aisle.' I had to walk away.

We went for our first visit to Whitemead for the weekend and whether Sophia felt there was a connection between Whitemead and Shelbie, I don't know, but she constantly talked about her. It was, 'Shelbie used to like lying in her bed, didn't she?' 'I don't want Shelbie to be gone forever.' 'Shelbie can't stay in Heaven forever, we need to see her.' 'Shelbie liked the park, didn't she, Nainy?' It was relentless (in fact, she still calls the swing in the park "Shelbie's swing") and it's strange how you think they'll forget, but they don't. Things in life are testing, and I strongly believe that everything happens for a reason. All that we go through, good and bad, is for us to learn from. What we take from it is our choice, so in a way we do get to choose the outcome.

Chapter Fourteen

August 2019. Four months on from Shelbie's promotion and we try to keep busy, but the days still feel empty. Maybe this is how it's always going to feel. Maybe that gap, that emptiness, makes sense because the person who filled it isn't here. We went for our annual long stay at Whitemead in the summer. Shelbie's special place. It was pretty tough but we still managed to have some laughs, as we had so many good memories, especially of Shelbie rolling away. For a few years running we stayed on the same pitch and there was a lovely tree that we would sit under when it got too hot, only Shelbie wanted to be under that tree all the time. It was past a slope from our caravan and, as soon as we put her outside on her blanket to have a roll around, she would be gone. I would go in the caravan to grab her toys and by the time I came back out she had rolled down the slope to the tree. We would bring her back up and off she would go again. It was unrelenting, but she loved doing it so we just went along with it, knackered from carrying her back up so many times.

During this stay my grandma — my dad's mum — was in hospital so we were going back and forth to visit her. Nothing unusual really as we had done the same at times with Shelbie just so the other kids' holiday wouldn't be ruined. Grandma had had a fall at home, then within days of being admitted had a major stroke and never recovered from it. I was very close to Grandma when the older ones were little because, as my parents had moved away for a few years, Grandma was always around for me. We got on really well and I could tell her anything. She had a brilliant sense of humour and we had quite a few giggles: we just seemed to get each other. When we were visiting her, I read some biblical words from a daily reading and played her some Christian music. I didn't want her always in silence and we knew she didn't have long left, so I wanted some of her last sounds to be encouraging for her. I was reading to her and it ran:

Are you ready to go home, are you ready to meet your loved ones, are you ready to meet your maker?'

That was the reading for that day. It hadn't been planned, but how apt it was. She then died the following day, a day before our holiday was due to end.

We went home the following day and prepared for my gran — my mum's mum — to come and stay for the week. My grandad had died from cancer the day after Shelbie, and he had been my gran's carer. She had COPD and anxiety disorder, so after he died, as a family, we all took over her care day and night. I was staying with her two nights a week and thoroughly enjoying it. Gran was the sweetest of people, as was Grandad, with a warming smile. I looked forward to her coming downstairs in the mornings as she was always wearing that sweet smile and it melted me every time. Once I had got her to bed at night (which was very late sometimes as we did like to chatter!) I would use the quiet time to sit and write about how I was feeling or what was going on with us as a family. It was quite therapeutic and caring for her was a welcome distraction from how quiet life had become at home.

We were having her to stay at ours so other family could go on holiday and not worry about who looked after her and when. She was coming to stay in Shelbs' room as it was all equipped for her. We were hoping to do a few days out with her, but she wasn't a hundred per cent so I got the GP out and he diagnosed a urinary tract infection. Apart from this, though, Gran had a good week. Our elderly friends, who are like family, came over to visit which Gran loved. That really brightened her up. Then Paul and Emma came over one evening which she enjoyed, followed by Matt and Laura with their kids the next evening.

Each night that I put Gran to bed, I would kiss her and she would always say, 'Goodnight darling, God bless.' On this particular evening I kissed her and she said, 'Goodnight darling, I love you.'

That threw me a bit, but I replied, 'Aww, I love you too.'

We checked on her throughout the night as usual. The following morning, Nick heard Gran moving around. She normally rang the bell for us to get her up, but on this occasion she didn't. Nick went into her and she said she needed the toilet but was heading to the armchair. Nick came and got me as she seemed a little confused, although she was talking OK. I went in to her and she had taken her O_2 off. Nick told me she kept doing that, which was a bit unusual. I wasn't getting much sense out of her and she couldn't stand. I tried giving her her inhaler, as she was breathless, I assumed from constantly removing her oxygen, but she refused it. She wasn't opening her eyes and was incoherent. I did some obs on her and her sats were very low and her feet and hands had gone blue. I realised that she was shutting down, so I called for an ambulance. She then lost consciousness and stopped taking any breaths. We managed to lie her on the bedroom floor, but it was no use. She had a DNAR — do not attempt resuscitation — so we couldn't do anything, and she was gone before the paramedics turned up. She died on Shelbie's bedroom floor, just four months after Shelbie herself had died.

It opened a lot of wounds back up for Nick. Our only comfort is how happy she is now and we feel blessed that she felt safe enough to go while she was with us. Every day since Grandad died, she wanted to go to sleep and not wake up. Not in a selfish way, but she felt she had done her time here — she had had a lovely life and now she just wanted to rest with her beloved husband. At last, she had her wish.

The following month was very draining with two funerals just a week apart.

The emptiness is no less, but we can talk more freely about Madam with less tears now.

I think Nick is holding onto it all more, as men often do, and it worries me that it's just all going to tumble out at once. We were unintentionally carrying on but moving apart. We weren't talking to each other about how we were feeling. I suppose when you talk, it's painful again, and we realised we were just ships passing. The communication had gone, something we had always been very good at. When we had all seven children at home as kids, once the last one had gone to bed, we would make some time, even if it was just an hour to sit and chat. That time on our own was important to us because of how crazy life was, so we made a conscious effort to do that and it seemed to work. We were tired but happy. But now, even just simple conversations were barely taking place.

Luckily, we recognised it, and we are trying to come together again. I guess there was a gap there anyway as soon as Shelbs went. She filled a space and with it suddenly being empty we hadn't realised we were heading in totally different directions. I'm praying that we can learn how to be together again without Shelbs in the middle, because, let's be fair, we've never known each other without her, so we need to start again and learn who these changed people are. We've both made it clear we love each other, so that's a start. I think we are getting there slowly. It's now been nearly seven months since Shelbie was promoted and in the last few weeks Nick has started talking so much more and it has sparked those conversations that no one wants to face. But in time that is going to heal us, not completely, ever, I don't think, but enough to one day function and be able to honour Shelbie by living life how she intended to live it and how she showed us to live it — to the absolute max. One day we won't be faking it. We will enjoy it for her and then I know she will definitely be smiling down on us.

Chapter Fifteen

November 2019… There are so many memories that I have been reminded of or that have bounced back these last few weeks, the weeks leading up to what would have been Shelbie's twentieth birthday. It's our first birthday without her and now these memories come flooding back. No doubt she has something to do with that. I found a note I had written about how I was feeling just a month ago. It read:

I can't believe it's nearly six months since we laid our little girl to rest. I don't mean the funeral — that was her celebration of life — I mean the day she took her last breath. That's when she rested. I have been sat in the car thinking about her funeral day and a lively song came on by Bethel called 'Raise A Hallelujah' and as the tears were about to start, I couldn't help but picture Shelbs up there in Heaven dancing and clapping with her chubby little hands to this music. Her huge grin and laughter.

So there are positive thoughts that come through and make me smile, give me a warm feeling of closeness to her.

Silly things come back to me. For example, while in PICU the children and I started learning to knit. We didn't get that far, to be honest, but we enjoyed it, and I would sit back up at Ronald Macdonald House after a long day and knit. I didn't realise how relaxing it could be, despite the numerous mistakes I would make.

And last Christmas, Gareth and Zoë brought us the best present ever: a cushion of Shelbie. We didn't realise how precious that cushion would be, and she takes pride of place in the middle of our sofa. I lie on it, thinking, 'This is the closest I will get to hugging her now.' When they gave us the gift (all nicely wrapped up) we put it under the tree and Shelbie took a real shine to it. She must have known it was about her, and she played with it under the tree more than she had played with any toy in a while, other than her bells. In the end, because she enjoyed playing with the parcel so much, once we'd unwrapped the gift, we had to replace it in the wrapping paper with an old cushion so that she could continue playing with it.

Another thing that used to make me laugh was Shelbie's amazing planning of when she would need an ambulance. You could guarantee that whenever we had to call one it was either when the house was a mess, we had friends over so it would get messy, or I'd decided to clear a cupboard out or sort through some clothes. It was never when the house was tidy. Once we were going to change Shelbie's room around. She was in bed, so I thought, right, while it's quiet, let's do it. Shelbie then became ill and the poor paramedics had to clamber over a pile of clothes and toys. It was almost as if she knew when it was the most inconvenient time to be ill. She did have a wicked sense of humour, and that's why she was such good company: she liked a bit of naughtiness!

Twenty-ninth November would have been her twentieth birthday. I thought I was doing OK until Paul and Emma bought Nick and I gifts for her birthday, things they wanted us to have before the day approached. The gave Nick a key ring with a lovely little quote on it, and I had something to go on Shelbie's Pandora bracelet that I wear — a verse from the Bible:

Do not fear, for I am with you. (Isaiah 41:10)

I didn't expect it to, but it brought on a flood of emotions. One simple little gesture, which I love and am so grateful for, stirred something up. I don't know if I had pushed my emotions further back than I had realised but they'd now been released. By the evening I was feeling quite emotional and a little unwell, and I woke up the next day full of cold, a headache and totally drained. I didn't realise how run down I was but I hadn't felt like this since those sleepless nights with Madam. Once that feeling came it made me feel like I was back in that time. Obviously, I'm not, but I wish I was.

We had decided to go to Whitemead for Shelbie's birthday because it was her favourite place, staying in the caravan for her despite it being the end of November! We had loads to get done before we left, so we popped to the supermarket and bumped into someone who we hadn't seen since

Shelbs had been promoted. When she started talking about her, I did OK, no tears. Then we went into the flower shop to get some balloons. I was fine until Nick came across some ornaments and little plaques with lovely little words on, especially the one that said, "Miss you sis", and I just lost it. I couldn't hold back the tears. After that we saw someone else who I knew in passing from the older kids being in school.

'I recognise you,' she said. 'You're the mum of that beautiful girl in the wheelchair, what's her name?' I told her and she said, 'That's right, I remember your other daughter [Courtney] zooming her around and I thought she's going to topple over in a minute.' I started laughing, and then she asked, 'How's she doing, anyway?' and I had to explain. All day I have just wanted to cry and feeling ill on top really didn't help. I just want to sleep and not wake up for about six months. It would be nice to fast forward from all the "firsts" and the pain you have to go through to get to that point, but that's not how it goes is it? Unless we feel the pain, we have no chance of starting to find our way into the new life we have to take up now.

On the eve of her birthday, I was sitting outside the caravan (everyone else was asleep) and it started to occur to me that the time I've been waiting for — that sudden realisation that Shelbie was gone — didn't really exist. You don't suddenly feel the penny drop followed by this relief that you're finally accepting it. I think this is just how it's going to feel. It will always seem surreal, like you're watching someone else's life going through it. I suppose you have to accept that you need to find a new way to live, knowing that's how you look on life now. I don't mean that necessarily in a negative way. It's not called a life changing situation for nothing, and it does change your life and change who you are. I can't ever be who I was before because when I was looking after Shelbs I was holding onto each and every day I had with her, and now all that has changed. So, I need to learn who the new me is now and take what I can from what Shelbie taught me to ensure that that is used for a greater good. I just have to work out how to start with that and how to use it. What is God's purpose for me now? He hasn't finished with me, He sent Shelbie for the first part of my lesson, and He has more He wants me to do. There are days I push the pain away because it hurts too much, there are other days I want to feel that pain because I need to try and make some kind of sense of what has happened. And there are days that I look forward to one day carrying Shelbs' message on, keeping her name alive for the benefit of others.

The next day was — would have been — Shelbie's twentieth birthday. We opened cards for her from Gareth and Zoë and, of course, from us. Nick had picked a fantastic card for her with words about how you tell your daughter how much you love her when you've seen her face so many challenges and overcome them. We told her constantly how proud we were of the way she fought her battles and I know that she knew what she meant to us. We sat together and read the cards, then the children went off swimming in her memory, while I took the dog for a walk through those same woods that Shelbs loved being pushed through. As I got deeper in there was a bright ray of sunshine coming through the trees. I thought, 'There you are, shining down on this cold day — the day twenty years ago on which I gave birth to you.'

We had hung up her bells back in her bed for the day, and Nick said, 'Round about now she would be in her bed playing with her bells while she went on the ventilator for a rest.' Hours later I realised that the time Nick had said that would have been, in fact, pretty much the time I was just giving birth to her. We put her balloons up in the bed ready to send to her tomorrow, then we all sat and watched endless videos of her on the TV and Nick had a drink of Guinness in her honour — her favourite drink. She has enjoyed Guinness and lager since she was about five as we always thought there was little point her having to wait as she may not get to eighteen. I remember once we were changing one of her meds and her doctor said, 'The only thing with this drug is you're not meant to drink on it, so just be careful how much she has.' She was eight at the time, so this was not a discussion that should have taken place, but it always made us laugh when we talked about it! In the evening we bought a new film to watch together and had a takeaway. There were often times over the years we had planned to go out for a meal and she wasn't quite up to it, so we would get a takeaway instead. And she always seemed happier with that, she loved us all being cosied up together, so it seemed quite fitting. It ended up being a good day really, but once everyone was asleep, I was left feeling an emptiness again. I looked at her bed and realised she would never lie in it again. It was all there for her — but not her herself.

The following day brought some kind of relief. I guess that sounds awful, but it had been so hard in the time leading up to it, there is so much pressure, and you don't know how you're going to feel on the day, how you're all going to cope, and you come to dread it. But Nick and I put the bench in place in between the park where you can see the swing she loved going on and the swimming pool which was her favourite place.

We then all went down with Shelbs' balloons, and Mac took the speech he had written for her. Loads of friends and family turned up to see it — there were about thirty people or so which meant the world to me: I was so chuffed. The children screwed the plaque onto the bench — this would have been about the time twenty years previously when I was getting ready to leave hospital with her — Mac did his speech then Cienna cut off one of the balloons and we wished it up to Shelbie, watching it soaring higher and higher. It was actually a really magical time and I hope Shelbie would have enjoyed it. Well, of course she would! It was all about her and she loved being the centre of attention so I think she would have been pleased with how the morning went. We all headed back up to the caravan and had sausage and bacon sandwiches and a hot drink, which we needed as it was so cold. Everyone sat around chatting and the children went off to play with their cousins. It was lovely that everyone had made such an effort, and it really meant a lot to me.

It's funny, because I hadn't talked much to God of late, not as much as I usually do. I just haven't been in a place where I have made time for Him and that's not really good enough. But despite that and because He is such a loving God, He sent a calmness to the day. There were a few tears but not that unbearable ache that I had expected. I didn't ask for it, yet He made the day more than bearable. Maybe that's my little push to start making more time for Him. After all, it's only because of His grace that I'm still standing right now, even He still gets me through even the hardest days. There's not a day that goes by that Shelbs isn't thought about or talked about, but it is often more bearable than I think it's going to be and for that I am grateful. I know it's only by the works of His hands that it's possible to feel like that.

The feeling from the weekend was short-lived, though. Once we got home the children wanted to put the Christmas decorations up, so we got out the trees and the tinsel, then all the lights. The lights were Shelbie's favourite part and that hit me so hard, I couldn't stop the tears. All the following week I have felt at quite a low. Even simple things like receiving Christmas cards, is hard, most people have just written to us a general, "Nick, Vic and family" which has been bearable but the children all received cards, obviously minus Shelbie, and it just hit home more than people could ever possibly imagine.

But we wanted to make Christmas as bearable for the children as we could, so we bought a Christmas ornament in memory of Shelbs and her love of lights and we have some meaningful little house and garden ornaments so the children can still open her presents for her as they've been used to. We also let them buy a little gift that will be meaningful to them for her, to go in her stocking (and we will do that each year so she can always have her stocking out with the others — thank you, Emma, for that idea).

With Christmas nearly upon us, and with everyone else talking about it, Mac turned to me in the kitchen one day and said, 'I don't want to do Christmas this year.' When I asked why, he replied that it would be too weird without Shelbie. 'It's the first Christmas we won't hear her crumpling up the wrapping paper. Things are no better. I feel so alone. A teacher said to me there's no time to be sad with GCSEs coming up. But I miss coming down in the morning and hearing her alarms, or her bells when she played with them, or seeing her sat in the conservatory having her breakfast.' I thought it was a terribly insensitive comment for that teacher to make and was quite annoyed by it. Mac had to deal with all this before he'd even made it to school. He'd known it all his life. No wonder it's tough.

Shelbie though was famous for loving her bells. She'd had them since she was three years old and anyone who knew her knew she loved them. Gareth bought her a cow bell to add onto her collection and we would buy various things as well. In hospital we would take them in and hang them on the hoists or wherever we could, and then we knew she would be happy when we weren't there.

As the weather has been getting colder as the winter drew on, I sat in my car one day and thought that Shelbs' leg would need to be wrapped up warmer, knowing that since her leg was broken, she suffered more with it in the cold. It's daft, isn't it, what comes to your mind for a split second and to think what the children's minds must go through at times.

Nick and I were sitting talking recently about films on the telly and I found myself starting to say, 'I'm going to make Shelbs watch a Christmas film with me this afternoon,' but stopped myself short, a few words in. We would often do that on a weekend afternoon, that or watch some singing contest that Madam liked. No one would watch them with me so I would drag Shelbs in, and she didn't care as long as she was cwtching with someone. So, result for me! I got to watch my film and have a cuddle at the same time. Mind you, if Shelbie really didn't like something she would soon let you know, so I think she must have enjoyed them too.

There was something said on a series we watch recently and I thought straight away of Shelbie when one of the characters said, 'I wanna keep fighting; endings be damned.' I think that's how Shelbie lived her life: she carried on fighting.

In the space of five years, I had four miscarriages in a row. The last one was when we were in and out of court for Sophia, and the emptiness I felt was numbing, but this is ten times worse. I realise though you never get to meet that baby or get to know them, hug them, kiss them, but I got all of that with Shelbie and much, much more. It's strange how life throws you in one corner, then another with totally different things, but they all come back to one thing: pain. Pain, and how you move on from it.

When Shelbie died, Dr Bruce said that in all his years he had never come across another child who had gone through so many up and downs. Not just going through them, but going from being so, so ill and then bouncing back as well as she did, often bouncing back to a better place than she had been before she was unwell. I had never thought about it before, but yes, she was made of steel, she really did seem indestructible, which I suppose is why everyone expected her to do it this last time, and why it was such a shock when she didn't. But it doesn't matter. She still made us proud of how long she did manage to fight and how she helped

241

teach us how to fight in life. She made us better people, and that has to make us determined not to stand down but to fight back, as she would have done. As she did, in fact, time and time again.

One of Shelbie's teachers, Craig, said to me that many times in school he would go looking for her, or would see something that reminds him of her. The feeling of loss is felt all round by all those who knew her.

We have a lot of headaches, tummy aches, and the like from Kalan, Mac and Cienna. Yes, kids do try to throw a sickie, but I think they just want to stay home where they feel safe and where they know we're around too. If I go anywhere, Kalan continuously rings to see where I am and how long I will be, something he never used to do. He also doesn't go out, preferring to sit with us on the sofa. He is nearly fifteen and should want to avoid his parents like the plague, like any other kid his age, but he seems to need that reassurance that we are here.

Cienna did manage to go on a guides' weekend and it did her a world of good, she even slept out at her friend's house after. Her little friend, Mollie, has been an absolute godsend, she has helped Cienna more than she'll ever realise, and we are so thankful she found such a good friend.

To some that have never experienced a loss in the way my children have, they wouldn't have the first idea what it must feel like. Losing a grandparent is devastating, losing my dad was heart-breaking, but to lose a sibling at their age must make their whole world feel so unsure. As I've said, we have always tried to teach them not to be frightened about death and dying, but when you are faced with it in the way they were, there have to be a lot of questions and a lot of insecurities.

Nick and I went to my aunty and uncle's house for the evening the other day and Nick said more on the way than he'd said in the last six or more months. He said how he hates driving, he misses her the most when he's driving because she used to come everywhere with us and even if she had school, we would be taking her or picking her up. He took her and Cie camping on his own a few times when I had been ill or had something on, and it had hit him that he could never do that again. He mentioned he was playing with Nellie, our granddaughter, and was encouraging her to sit up by pulling her arms up, and halfway through he remembered doing that with Shelbie. In fact, he used to clap to Shelbs and say, 'Up' and she would clap back and reach her arms out. If she wouldn't do it, he would say, 'I'm not lifting you up then,' and then she would comply. He said he just wanted to drop Nellie back down, but realised he couldn't. It wasn't her fault it was so painful. He said he found it hard to play with her sometimes, feeling guilty because he's not playing with Shelbs and also didn't want Shelbs to feel she'd been replaced.

Nick also said he absolutely hated weekends. Weekdays are all right because Shelbie was often at school anyway. I feel the same too. Sunday afternoon always had a pattern: check Shelbie's button, change her syringes, clean her O_2 concentrator, check and change as necessary her ventilating tubes, and so on. Now, after church, there is nothing. Saturdays drag too. And there's also such a feeling of guilt. It has been refreshing talking about all these things. We did it again today when we went out, so hopefully we'll keep doing it and I think the guilt will get less and less. Shelbie was jealous whenever Nick gave attention to anyone else, but she won't be like that now. She will be happy that we can still give love to others, because she was sent to give us that ability and she knows she has done that job and so she can be happy for us. We just need to learn how to use that. Looking at the positives, we do have a lot of love and we will continue to share that, hopefully with children who need it for whatever reason. It doesn't matter if they're not our blood children. We can love whoever needs to be loved, and in the not-so-distant future we will welcome children into our home in honour of our little girl, and we will carry on the lessons she has taught us, the biggest of which is acceptance.

You should never assume that just because a person is born different it's a bad thing — a bit tougher maybe, but not bad. It's mainly people's attitudes that make it tougher for them, much more so than their condition. Every person has a right to be different. If ever you're blessed with a child with special needs, embrace it. Don't feel your journey is over. You're just on a different journey down a different road than you had originally planned, and you'll learn different — and probably better — things along the way.

Although days are painful, I sometimes feel a real calm, peace even, and I know that God is doing that as he's carrying me. I believe that Shelbie has a lot to do with it too, in what she made me over the years, what she gave me. The memories she's left me give me comfort, and although she also gave me some worrying times, even during those days we managed to find humour, and even those memories are a comfort and make me laugh. And we have some fantastic friends that we would never have met without her. She was special, unique, kind, funny, clever and, most of all, selfless. So much to give, and only asking for acceptance back. What a character, what a person, what a life!

Life

I sit and stare on a bright sunny day,
The birds flying by
We know not when all this comes to an end
When we have to say goodbye.

But thank God for every breath
For every day we see
Life is an amazing gift
A gift from you to me.

You've helped me through so much my friend
To see each day anew
And only you, my Lord, decides
If I stay or go — if I'm meant to.

Whatever our tomorrow brings
I say dear Lord, thank you
For you showed me the way, you gave me this life
I will use it how you wanted me to.

Afterword — February 2020

It's been nearly a year, and we've been talking about what we will do come the first anniversary of Shelbie being promoted.

This week we watched the new series of *Born To Be Different*, the TV programme we are in, or, to be more accurate, were in. It will be aired in about four weeks' time and the production company came round so that we could see what would be going out. It's very well done but it was so, so difficult to watch. It hit us all harder than we thought it would, especially the children. In fact, in some ways I think it re-opened some wounds for us. Kalan really struggled and I realised he just wasn't getting enough support, so I have contacted a charity that can hopefully help him. He has tried to do it alone and in the way he thinks will help him cope, but they are all so young. How can they know how to deal with this loss, how can they process and break down such an enormous sadness that has happened in their lives? We still feel so alone and lost at times, and we are adults. How can a child come to terms with all that has happened?

There are periods where I feel I'm OK and I'm coming to terms, if you like, with what has happened, but then there are other times when it feels just as raw as if it happened just a few days ago. I am dreading that first anniversary coming up because I think, after that first year, that's when people expect you to have moved on and as time passes less and less is said about the person who has died. They think that as time goes by, you will mention and think about them less and less. I'm not ready for that. I want to keep the memories alive. I think because of who Shelbie was, she deserves to be remembered over and over and over. I want to get out there and keep talking about her life and keep teaching what she taught. I don't really know how to do that, but I feel I owe it to her to keep her endless love alive. My fibromyalgia has really flared up this week and I've realised how run down I am and how hard watching *Born To Be Different* was. It's just two months until Shelbie's anniversary and I know the way forwards is to honour her purpose in life. I think I know what that means and what I have to do, but then I start questioning what I'm actually doing. The general day-to-day running of the house goes on, of course, and it still manages to be as manic as ever, but knowing what is needed of me and where I go next is less clear. I still want to help other families and children like Shelbie. I didn't amass nineteen years of medical training just for it to be wasted now, but I'm just not sure what I do with it, or where I should take it.

I will never feel alive again in that part of me has died with Shelbs, and I think Nick feels the same. I don't think a lot of people realise the impact it has on your life. I just don't think they get how different everything is now and forever will be. Connor has been staying with us for a while, but he is really struggling. It is heart-breaking seeing a nearly twenty-four-year-old looking so lost, like a child who is scared to go to school on their first day without you. That look of not knowing what to expect or how to cope with it alone. He is now getting support but it's going to be a long road for him, as it will be with the others, and that's what I think some people don't get. It's not a quick fix, or a few months of crying and we all just move on; it could take years for all of the children to come to terms with this situation.

But there are positives too. Cienna came home from school today and said, 'Look, Mum, I have a letter saying I'm not in the amber for my school attendance. I've actually got a hundred per cent. That's the first time since I started school!' We would get letters every however many months, reminding us of how much time the children had missed off school and that it would send them into the amber zone, which obviously wasn't good, and which Cienna hated, but we couldn't help them having that time off when Shelbs was ill in hospital or we were all at the children's hospice. So, when she brought the letter home, I should have been happy for once. But then again, I knew the reason she wasn't in the amber zone any longer was because Shelbie wasn't here, and so it actually made me a little sad. While I always appreciated that education is important, it could never be more important than family. Being together and making memories was always significant and for me there will never be any regret over that.

We have also had weather warnings for snow. I usually love the snow, but I am actually dreading it, as it will be the first snowfall since Shelbie left us. These things don't really get easier. Each time something else comes up it just becomes harder, and I imagine it's just going to be this way for ever. There will be times when we feel positive and times when we feel down and it's recognising that that's normal and that it's OK to feel that way. And that's not being negative, it's just to try to help others to understand that this is how up and down life is for us as a family.

We are not going to apologise for the feelings we have, but we will try our damn hardest to carry on dealing with all of this as a family. We will try carrying each other and so not have to do it alone, and as long as we do that Shelbie will be happy that we are all still together. The most important thing to her was her family. She loved her family. Whenever she was ill in hospital, she needed them around her. They were her tonic, and she would want to know that if she can't be with us all, then at least she would want us to be around for each other. That's what family would mean to her. I don't mind whatever my children want to do in their lives, or with their lives. I just like to think they are happy and can enjoy being alive and accepting and giving love so freely, just as their sister did. She is the best example I have ever been shown of what good and pure looks like.

For now, we'll carry on, hopefully doing Shelbie proud by living by her example, and if I can just give half the love Shelbie gave and be half the child of God she was, then when my time comes, I will die knowing I carried on where she left off. And because of how she taught me to live, I too will be going to Heaven, and one day I will not only be with my girl again, but I will also get to spend forever with my boy, Charlie, after our time together was so short the first time around. So, I am just going to try and live by my daughter's example, the girl with the most beautiful heart I have ever met and will ever meet.

Thank you, God, for choosing us, then blessing us for so long with our contagious, inspiring, daft comical child — the little girl who loved the song 'Happy Birthday' even when it wasn't her birthday.

You truly changed our lives for the better, and we love you so much, Shelbie Eloise.

Shelbie 13.04.2020

by Esther Townsend

I never knew you from the start,
Shelbie Eloise
It wasn't 'til you were a tot
You whooshed in like a breeze.

I met my man and soon enough
We'd been introduced
A smiley, happy, funny girl,
Joyful and footloose.

I say footloose because my dear
Quite quickly I realised
A face too near to Shelbie
Meant a kick right in the eyes.

I didn't know how to talk to you
Or what you understood
But your mum quickly told me
'She knows much more than she should!'

She showed me how you loved to play
To wrestle and to clap
And how you loved your music
Amy Grant, Westlife, Take That.

I sang to you when I could
To help us to engage
You'd pull my hair and listen in
And sometimes you would praise.

I knew we had connection
Even though you didn't speak

Your noises meant the world to me
Even your kicking feet.

We watched you grow and soon enough
You turned from child to teen
A brave courageous fighter girl
The best I've ever seen.

You never let it hold you back
You kept on pushing deep
To find the strength and carry on
And sometimes even sleep!

But as you grew the battle scars
Grew thicker with each dip
And slowly as you tired, my love
We knew away you'd slip.

We didn't know when that would be
We wanted you to choose
But breathing was a battle
We knew eventually you'd lose.

Although it came so peacefully
For that we all agree
It was in fact a peaceful time
To watch you run so free.

You waited 'til you saw him
At those golden shiny gates
And off you ran into his arms
For Jesus, He awaits.

So now a year has come and gone
We miss you oh so much
Dear Shelbie we will always miss

Your strong affirming touch!

We'll cherish every rainbow
Every bubble in the sky
For that's how I'll remember you
Footloose and riding high.

I hope you sing and talk all day
And dance before His feet
We miss you Shelbie Eloise
Until in Heaven we will meet.

On Shelbie's Twentieth Birthday

Happy birthday, darling girl, you had to go before this day
There's nothing that can part our love, the bond will always stay
I close my eyes and feel your skin, your smell I try to relive
Just one more time to have all that, there's nothing I wouldn't give

But nearly twenty years we had of love and hope and smiles
They're still being given out I'm sure, it matters not the miles
Your smile is in every breath I take, I feel your radiance still
I'll carry on for you because you're my strength, my heart and my will

Your freedom's there and you earned it tenfold, go laugh and run and play
There isn't a moment I think it was wrong for you to go on that beautiful day
It breaks my heart I can't hold out my arms and feel you cwtching right there
But to keep you longer when you could feel pain wasn't right, that just wasn't fair

Thank you precious for all you gave, for the battles you won to be near
I'll never forget having you in our lives, those memories will always be here
You're a treasure that God had decided to loan and I thank Him for choosing me
I thank Him for showing the rest of the world that brave heart that we all could see

To end this now, all I can say is I thank you for being with us
I'd do it again, I'd fight that fight as you taught — just do it, no fuss
I'll see you again, that I don't doubt, but 'til then I'll spread your word
To show others to accept, to give love and forgive, your message will still be heard.